AWESOME

Edible

KIDS CRAFTS

75 SUPER-FUN
ALL-NATURAL PROJECTS
FOR KIDS TO MAKE AND EAT

ARENA BLAKE

FOUNDER OF THE NERD'S WIFE

PAGE STREET
PUBLISHING CO.

For Andrew,

MAY YOU NEVER BE TOO OLD TO
PLAY WITH YOUR FOOD.

PAGE STREET
PUBLISHING CO.

Contents

Introduction

From a young age, we are taught to never play with our food. It's bad manners, grown-ups tell us. The dinner table is a place to sit up straight and use our forks! (Can you hear your grown-up saying that?)

Well, I'm here to ask that we set aside those rules, just for a little while. It's fun to play. And it's fun to play with food.

I mean, what's more fun than building a rocket ship? How about building a rocket ship and THEN EATING IT? Yum. That is what we're going to do in this book. *Awesome Edible Kids Crafts* explores ways to make food fun.

My love of cooking first surfaced when I won a blue ribbon at the local county fair for my homemade broccoli cheese soup. The pride I felt at creating something that others could enjoy was an emotion my young heart seized upon. I was hooked.

Some of my favorite childhood memories involve baking with my mom, or learning to cook from my grandmother. I once convinced a classmate in college that we should design a logo for a restaurant as our marketing project just so I could make tapas. My apartment smelled like garlic for weeks afterward.

That's what I love most about cooking and crafting. The adventure. The unknown. Figuring out the process and imagining what you can create. Many of the projects found in this book came about by trial and error. Testing and trying. Building and failing. But then succeeding. And that is the fun of it all.

In our time together, you will find out how to make squishy playdough that's good enough to eat, crackers that sparkle with your own constellations and cookies that you can color. You will be immersed in play so fun that it is only limited by your imagination.

Are you ready? Let's get to cooking.

Jenna Blake

Let's Play

Have you ever wondered what happens when you melt gummy bears in the microwave? In this chapter, we're going to find out.

The next few pages feature some of my favorite recipes that have one purpose—to play.

We're going to turn marshmallows into playdough and cereal into art. Then we'll paint our breakfast and make some crayons you can eat. Oh, and we'll make some fun jewelry for our friends along the way.

Are you ready to play?

MARSHMALLOW PLAYDOUGH

Playdough is one of the best ways to stretch your imagination. Build a city, create animals or cut out fun shapes—the sky is the limit!

But this playdough is special. You can eat it! So build to your heart's content, then enjoy a yummy treat.

INGREDIENTS

FOR EACH COLOR OF PLAYDOUGH, YOU WILL NEED

6 jumbo marshmallows

1 tbsp (14 g) coconut oil

5 tbsp (40 g) confectioners' sugar, plus more for kneading

4 drops food coloring

EQUIPMENT

Microwave-safe bowl

Microwave

Oven mitts

Spoon

Cutting board

Place the marshmallows, coconut oil and confectioners' sugar in a microwave-safe bowl, separating them as much as possible. Drop the food coloring directly onto the marshmallows to make it easier to mix.

Microwave for 15 to 30 seconds, until the marshmallows start to grow. Use oven mitts to carefully remove the bowl from the microwave—it's hot!

Stir the ingredients together. They'll be very sticky at first but as you stir, they will start to come together and pull away from the sides of the bowl.

Coat your hands in confectioners' sugar and remove the mixture from the bowl. Place it on a cutting board. Knead with your hands, adding more confectioners' sugar as you go to make the playdough less sticky.

Repeat with more colors until you are ready to play!

Store in an airtight container. The playdough will only last a few days, so enjoy it while you can.

DID YOU KNOW?

Ancient Egyptians were the first to enjoy marshmallows, as early as 2000 BCE.

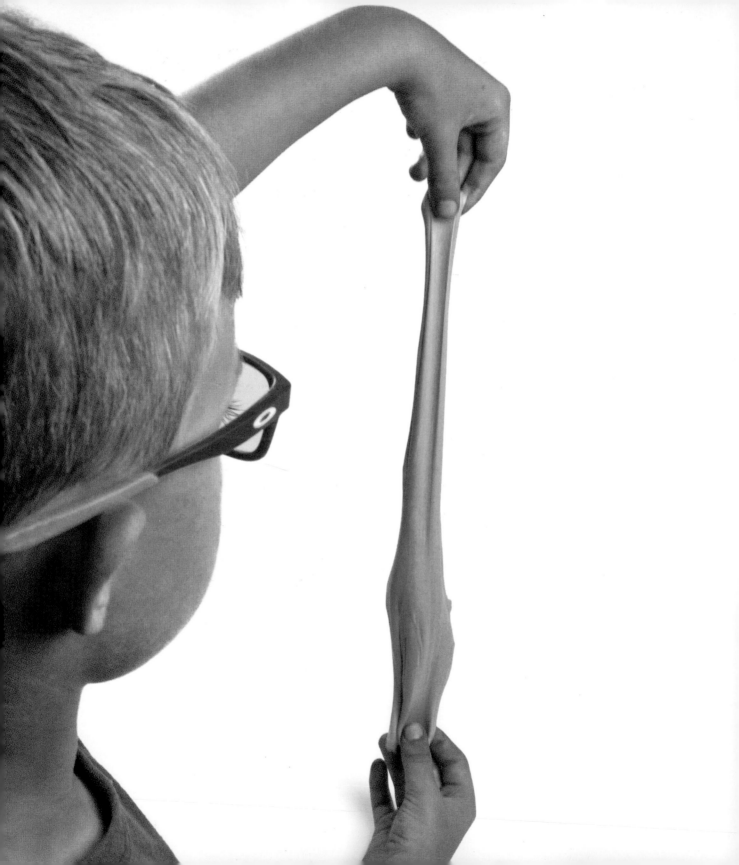

ADULT SUPERVISION
REQUIRED

MODERATELY EASY

INGREDIENTS

1 cup (225 g) gummy
bears

2 tbsp (16 g) cornstarch

1 tbsp (8 g)
confectioners' sugar

1 tsp oil

EQUIPMENT

Microwave-safe bowl

Microwave

Spoon

Oven mitts

Small bowl

Cutting board

GUMMY BEAR SLIME

Ooey, gooey slime is a great way to engage your senses. Watch it stretch, feel it twist, listen to it crunch, smell the ingredients and even taste this sticky concoction.

So grab a bag of gummy bears and enjoy this fun sensory play activity.

Sort the gummy bears by color, then add 1 cup (225 g) of similarly colored bears to a microwave-safe bowl.

Microwave on high for 30 seconds, then stir. Use oven mitts to carefully remove the bowl from the microwave—it's hot! Reheat as needed, stirring after each time, until the mixture is smooth and no bear parts remain.

Mix the cornstarch and confectioners' sugar together in a small bowl. Place half the mixture onto a cutting board, then pour the melted gummy bears onto it. Add the remaining cornstarch/sugar mixture on top.

Once the mixture is cool enough to touch, knead it together until all the ingredients are incorporated. Add the oil to the mixture to make it more stretchy and pliable.

This Gummy Bear Slime is a one-use recipe, so get as much play as you can out of it!

DID YOU KNOW?
Some green gummy bears are strawberry flavored!

EDIBLE SAND ART

You don't have to head to the beach to make this colorful sand art. In fact, you can just grab your favorite sugary cereal. Here, vibrant layers of color combine for a unique piece of art. And the best part? When you're finished, you can pour in some milk and enjoy a yummy breakfast.

NO ADULT SUPERVISION
REQUIRED

EASY

INGREDIENTS

1 (17-oz [482-g]) box sugar cereal (I used Froot Loops)

EQUIPMENT

Plastic zip-top bags

Rolling pin

Funnel

Clear bowl or jar

Sort the cereal by color and place it into zip-top bags. Use the rolling pin to crush the cereal until it looks like colored sand. If your grown-up has a food processor, you can ask for help crushing the cereal, but I think it's more fun to smash it!

Use a funnel to pour your cereal into a clear container, layering the colors to make designs.

DID YOU KNOW?
The color of sand is determined by the material it's made of. Black sand is made from tiny bits of volcanic rock. White sand is made from bits of limestone. Yellow sand is colored by quartz rock with tiny imperfections.

GET CREATIVE!
What happens if you mix colors of your edible sand? Can you create a new color by combining blue and red? What about blue and yellow? What happens if you mix all the colors together?

ADULT SUPERVISION MAY
BE REQUIRED

MODERATELY HARD

INGREDIENTS

1 cup (200 g) granulated
sugar

1 cup (225 g) unsalted
butter

1 egg

1½ tsp (7 ml) almond
extract

3 cups (375 g) all-
purpose flour

1½ tsp (6 g) baking
powder

½ tsp salt

4 cups (480 g)
confectioners' sugar

3 tbsp (24 g) meringue
powder

5 tbsp (75 ml) warm
water

EQUIPMENT

Bowls

Mixer

Spoon

Oven

Baking sheet

COLORING BOOK COOKIES

There's nothing better than a blank canvas to use your imagination. And when that canvas is a sweet and delicious cookie? Now that's art worth sharing.

Parchment paper

Rolling pin

Square cookie cutter

Oven mitts

Edible food markers

MAKE YOUR OWN SUGAR COOKIES

Cream the granulated sugar and butter together in a mixer on high. Add the egg and almond extract and mix to combine. In a separate bowl, whisk together the flour, baking powder and salt. Slowly mix in the dry ingredients until a dough forms. Chill the dough for 1 hour.

Preheat the oven to 350°F (180°C). Line a baking sheet with parchment paper. On a lightly floured surface, roll out the dough to your desired thickness (¼ inch [6 mm] is standard). Use the square cookie cutter to cut the dough. Transfer to the baking sheet and bake for 6 to 10 minutes, or until lightly golden. Remove from oven with oven mitts. Allow to cool completely before icing.

MAKE YOUR OWN ROYAL ICING

In a mixing bowl, beat the confectioners' sugar, meringue powder and water together until peaks form.

ASSEMBLE THE COOKIES

Trace the outline of your cookies with the royal icing. Add water to thin the icing, then flood the inside of the cookie with it. Allow it to dry for 24 hours so the icing will harden.

Use the edible food markers to color your cookies. What will you draw? Maybe your family? Or a special message for a friend? There are so many possibilities!

DID YOU KNOW?
Settlers in Pennsylvania created the modern version of the sugar cookie in the 1700s.

PAINTED RAINBOW TOAST

Breakfast has never looked so good! Take boring old toast to the next level with edible milk paint. You can add rainbow stripes to your bread, like we did, or even draw a picture for your grown-up!

NO ADULT SUPERVISION
REQUIRED

MODERATELY EASY

INGREDIENTS

1½ cups (355 ml) milk, divided

Blue food coloring

Red food coloring

Yellow food coloring

Green food coloring

Bread

EQUIPMENT

6 small containers

Spoon

Paintbrushes

Toaster

Pour ¼ cup (60 ml) of milk into each of the 6 small containers.

Add a couple drops of food coloring to each container and stir to mix well (see the color chart). This is your edible paint!

Paint designs onto the bread using a paintbrush. Allow it to dry for 30 minutes before heating in a toaster. Serve warm.

COLOR MIXING GUIDE

Purple	1 drop red + 1 drop blue
Pinkish red	2 drops red
Orange	1 drop red + 1 drop yellow
Yellow	2 drops yellow
Green	2 drops green
Blue	2 drops blue

DID YOU KNOW?

French toast isn't actually toast! That's because it's the egg coating on French toast that is cooked, not the actual bread itself.

ADULT SUPERVISION
REQUIRED

MODERATELY EASY

JELLY BEAN BRACELETS

When I was a little girl, I begged my mom to buy me one of those pasty-looking candy bracelets at the grocery store. Have you seen those? The candy is hard, and it tastes horrible. Definitely NOT the kind of candy bracelet my young heart desired.

But these jelly bean bracelets are so much better. Coordinate them with your outfits and no one will know you have a yummy treat for later.

INGREDIENTS

1 cup (240 g) jelly beans

EQUIPMENT

Scissors

Stretchy beading cord

Embroidery needle with large eye

Sort the jelly beans by color to make designing your bracelets easier. Cut some beading cord about 2 inches (5 cm) longer than the length your bracelet should be. Tie a knot in one end, then thread the beading cord onto the embroidery needle.

Push the needle through a jelly bean, threading it onto the bracelet. Add more jelly beans, creating patterns with the colors.

When your bracelet is full, tie the two cord ends together and slip it onto your wrist!

> ### DID YOU KNOW?
> It takes 7 to 21 days to make a jelly bean!

WOVEN CANDY FRIENDSHIP BRACELETS

Friendship bracelets were all the rage when I was growing up. I remember trying tons of different ways to braid them and tie them. Oh boy, was that fun.

But these friendship bracelets are even better because they're made with candy. That's right. You are going to be the most popular friend in school when your classmates learn just how awesome your candy braiding skills are.

INGREDIENTS

4 fun-sized pieces of sheet candy, such as Airheads, in varying colors

EQUIPMENT

Cutting board

Rolling pin

Sharp knife

Unwrap the sheet candy, place it on a cutting board and use a rolling pin to stretch each piece. Cut the pieces into thin threads using a sharp knife. Press the ends of 3 different colors together and braid the threads of candy.

If you run out of one color, press another thread of that color to the end of the first, and continue braiding.

Your finished bracelet should be 6 to 8 inches (15 to 20 cm) long. Press the ends together to finish it off.

DID YOU KNOW?

Tradition says you should give a friendship bracelet to someone who has a wish. They should wear it until it falls off, and when it does, their wish will be granted!

EDIBLE CRAYONS

Crayons are probably my favorite art supply. There are so many things you can do with them—color, draw or write! Or melt them down and make wax art. Color over them with black and scratch out a design. The possibilities are endless.

These crayons are so much cooler, because they're made of candy. And they really color. Now that's awesome.

ADULT SUPERVISION
REQUIRED

MODERATE

INGREDIENTS

¼ cup (20 g) candy melts for each crayon

EQUIPMENT

6 milkshake straws

Masking tape

Nonstick cooking spray

Microwave-safe bowl

Microwave

Oven mitts

Cup

Small funnel

Bamboo skewer or thin dowel

Knife

Pencil sharpener

Jumbo crayon wrappers (optional)

Gather 6 milkshake straws into a bunch and wrap it in masking tape to hold in place. Spray the inside of each straw with nonstick cooking spray.

In a microwave-safe bowl, prepare the candy melts according to the package directions until they are smooth and runny. Remove from the microwave with oven mitts—the bowl will be hot! Place the prepared straws into a cup so they will stand upright. Use a funnel to pour each color of melted candy into its own straw. Allow to harden.

When they're ready to remove, press the end of a bamboo skewer or dowel into the straw to push the candy crayon out of it. Use the knife to cut the candy crayon to size, then sharpen the end using the pencil sharpener.

Wrap the finished crayons in the crayon wrappers so they look like actual crayons. These would be perfect for an art party!

GET CREATIVE!

Draw on rice paper to create completely edible drawings! Make a card for a friend, or a picture you can share with a grown-up.

DID YOU KNOW?

The average child goes through 720 crayons by his or her 10th birthday.

CHOCOLATE CHIP COOKIE PLAYDOUGH

Have you ever wanted to try raw cookie dough, but your grown-ups said it might make you sick? Something about raw eggs.

Well, this chocolate chip cookie playdough tastes just like real cookie dough, except it doesn't have any eggs. So play with it, build with it, then try a bite.

NO ADULT SUPERVISION REQUIRED

MODERATELY EASY

INGREDIENTS

2 tbsp (28 g) unsalted butter, softened

¼ cup (60 g) brown sugar

2 drops vanilla extract

Pinch of salt

1½ tsp (7 ml) milk

4 tbsp (30 g) all-purpose flour

¼ cup (45 g) chocolate chips

EQUIPMENT

Small bowl

Fork

Mix the butter, brown sugar, vanilla extract and salt in a small bowl. Add the milk and combine with a fork until the mixture comes together. Pour in the flour 1 tablespoon (8 g) at a time and mix until a dough forms. Knead in the chocolate chips with your hands.

Now your dough is ready to play with! Use extra chocolate chips to decorate the tops of your creations before chowing down on this super yummy snack!

DID YOU KNOW?

The chocolate chip cookie was created by accident! The creator added broken pieces of chocolate bars to her cookie recipe, thinking they would melt. When they didn't, chocolate chip cookies were born.

EDIBLE KINETIC SAND

NO ADULT SUPERVISION
REQUIRED

MODERATELY EASY

Kinetic sand is one of the coolest substances on the planet. Sometimes it acts like a solid. Sometimes it acts like a liquid. And it's super fun to just run your fingers through.

The best part? This edible version of kinetic sand tastes like hot chocolate. Yum.

INGREDIENTS

4 cups (500 g) all-purpose flour

1 cup (235 ml) oil (vegetable or canola oil)

4 tbsp (30 g) hot chocolate powder

EQUIPMENT

Large bowl

Fork

Mix the flour and oil in a large bowl. Add in the hot chocolate powder. Stir together for kinetic sand that can be squished, built and molded.

DID YOU KNOW?

Kinetic sand is made up of sand that's been coated in a substance that causes the sand to only stick to itself. This viscoelasticity makes the sand seem to move over time, but keeps it from feeling sticky.

MARSHMALLOW PAINT

Have you ever wished your sandwich had a little more color? Or your cookie said your name? Maybe you wanted red graham crackers instead of boring brown.

That's where this marshmallow paint recipe comes in. Mix up a batch and see what you can paint.

ADULT SUPERVISION
REQUIRED

MODERATELY EASY

INGREDIENTS

1 cup (45 g) mini marshmallows

¼ cup (60 ml) water

3 tbsp (65 g) light corn syrup

Food coloring

EQUIPMENT

Microwave-safe bowl

Microwave

Oven mitts

Spoon

Small bowls

Place the mini marshmallows in a microwave-safe bowl and heat on high for 30 seconds. Use oven mitts to carefully remove the bowl from the microwave—it's hot! Stir in the water and heat on high for 30 more seconds. Mix until it is smooth, then stir in the corn syrup.

Separate into small bowls and allow to cool. Add a few drops of food coloring to each bowl to make different colored paints.

Use your marshmallow paint to decorate graham crackers, cookies or even rice paper.

DID YOU KNOW?
The Greek philosopher Plato first discovered you can mix two colors of paint to make a third color.

Party Time

Don't you just love a party? Decorations, games, music—it's a time for celebration and FUN. Throw in a few treats and your celebration becomes one for the record books.

In this chapter, I've put together everything you need to throw a fabulous party, and the best part is . . . every project is edible. From the party banner to the balloons, these treats can be enjoyed by all. Yum.

ADULT SUPERVISION
REQUIRED

HARD

EDIBLE TAFFY BALLOONS

Wait, what? Edible balloons? They just might be the coolest party decoration ever. Fill them with helium for a one-of-a-kind party decoration.

So grab a grown-up—you'll need their help, trust me—and get this party started!

INGREDIENTS

½ cup (120 ml) plus 2 tbsp (30 ml) water, divided

1 tbsp (7 g) unflavored gelatin

1 cup (200 g) sugar

2 tbsp (16 g) cornstarch

⅔ cup (225 g) light corn syrup

½ tsp salt

EQUIPMENT

Small bowl

Spoon

Saucepan

Stove

Food thermometer

Vinyl tubing

Helium tank

Masking tape

String

In a small bowl, stir 2 tablespoons (30 ml) of the water into the gelatin powder until well combined. Set aside.

In a medium saucepan, mix together the sugar, cornstarch, corn syrup, remaining ½ cup (120 ml) of water and the salt over medium-high heat. Bring to a boil, stirring constantly.

Heat the mixture until it reaches 255°F (124°C) on the food thermometer, then remove from the heat. Carefully stir in the gelatin mixture.

Attach one end of the tubing to the helium tank using masking tape. Cover the other end of the tubing with the sugar mixture. Slowly turn on the helium tank, allowing the mixture to expand and your balloon to fill with helium. You can also blow it up by attaching the taffy to a straw, but it will be a little droopy.

As the balloon expands, wrap the string around the bottom of the mixture to detach the balloon from the tube.

DID YOU KNOW?

When a latex balloon pops, the noise breaks the sound barrier!

ADULT SUPERVISION
REQUIRED

●●●○○

MODERATE

GELATIN CUPS

Wiggly, jiggly and awesome, these gelatin cups would be great for a party or just an afternoon snack. Add patterns by layering different colors, or make a bunch of solid-colored cups for a kaleidoscope display.

Drinks are always more fun when you can enjoy them in a cool cup!

INGREDIENTS

3 (6-oz [170-g]) packages flavored gelatin, different colors

9 oz (255 g) unflavored gelatin, divided

1¼ cups (296 ml) hot water, divided

EQUIPMENT

3 heatproof bowls

Spoon

Hole punch

6 (18-oz [532-ml]) plastic cups

6 (9-oz [266-ml]) plastic cups

12 bamboo skewers

Scissors

Pour the 3 flavored gelatins into their own bowls. In each bowl, pour one-third of the unflavored gelatin. Pour one-third of the water into each bowl and mix well. Do not let it set.

Punch 4 holes around the outer rim of each cup, so you can create a cross pattern. Pour the gelatin into each one of the 18-ounce (532-ml) cups until each is about three-fourths full. Press a 9-ounce (266-ml) cup into each 18-ounce (532-ml) cup. The gelatin should rise to the top of the cup.

Thread 2 bamboo skewers across the holes in an X to hold the cups in place (see photo below). Repeat with the remaining cups. You should have 2 cups of each color gelatin for a total of 6 cups.

Allow the gelatin cups to set, then remove the bamboo skewers and cut the cups away for a wiggly, edible cup that is perfect for parties!

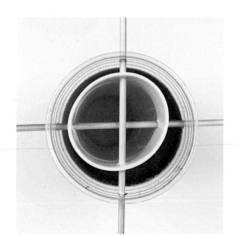

DID YOU KNOW?

In the early 1900s, immigrants arriving at Ellis Island in New York were given free samples of Jell-O. For many, it was their first taste of America!

ADULT SUPERVISION
REQUIRED

MODERATE

CHOCOLATE SPRINKLE BOWLS

There's nothing better than chocolate . . . except maybe a bowl made out of it!

Fill these chocolate sprinkle bowls with ice cream, fruit or any other snack for a treat that is as impressive as it is fun. And the best part is that you don't have to do the dishes after.

INGREDIENTS

1 cup (80 g) chocolate candy melts

½ cup (80 g) sprinkles

EQUIPMENT

Microwave-safe bowl

Microwave

Oven mitts

6 balloons

Wax paper

In a microwave-safe bowl, prepare the candy melts according to the package directions until they are smooth and runny. Remove from the microwave with oven mitts—the bowl will be hot!

Allow it to cool enough so it is safe to touch but still pliable. Blow up a balloon and dip it in the chocolate. Coat it in sprinkles, then place on a sheet of wax paper to harden.

Once the chocolate has hardened, pop the balloon and remove it from the chocolate shell.

Fill the shell with ice cream, whipped cream and fruit, or any other fun snack!

DID YOU KNOW?
During the Revolutionary War, soldiers were sometimes paid in chocolate.

NO ADULT SUPERVISION REQUIRED

EASY

EDIBLE PAPER CONFETTI

What's a party without confetti? Make some of your own with this simple project. Mix colors together or make an ombre effect for a unique twist on traditional confetti. You can even customize your edible paper confetti to match your party colors and theme.

INGREDIENTS

4 sheets rice paper

Edible spray food coloring

EQUIPMENT

Wax paper

Scissors

Spread the rice paper onto the wax paper and spray the colors onto it. Allow to dry completely.

Cut into squares and use for party confetti!

GET CREATIVE!

You can also use edible markers to draw on the rice paper. Write a message in the confetti for your party guests!

DID YOU KNOW?

Confetti was first used on New Year's Eve in 1881 in Paris, France.

NO ADULT SUPERVISION
REQUIRED

MODERATELY EASY

BIRTHDAY CAKE PLAYDOUGH

Forget birthday cake, let's make some birthday cake playdough! Mold it into your favorite party treat, roll it out and build something cool, then grab a piece and enjoy a snack. This soft, fluffy playdough tastes just like birthday cake.

INGREDIENTS

1 (16-oz [455-g]) can vanilla cake frosting

1½ cups (180 g) confectioners' sugar

¾ cup (90 g) all-purpose flour

Rainbow sprinkles

EQUIPMENT

Spoon

Large bowl

Scoop the frosting into a large bowl. Stir in the confectioners' sugar and flour until the mixture thickens, then use your hands to knead the dough until it becomes smooth.

Pour in the sprinkles and work them through the playdough with your hands.

Now you can build with the playdough and when you're done, you can eat it!

This playdough is good for a onetime use.

DID YOU KNOW?
"Happy Birthday to You" is the most frequently sung song in the English language.

EDIBLE PARTY HATS

MODERATE

Make a build-a-hat station at your next birthday party for a treat that your guests will love to wear—and eat! Or grab some friends and have a tea party with edible hats. Pretend it's crazy hat day and make hats for your whole family, including your pet. Now wouldn't they look cool with an ice cream cone hat?

INGREDIENTS

¼ cup (20 g) candy melts in varying colors

1 waffle ice cream cone

Sprinkles

EQUIPMENT

Microwave-safe bowl

Microwave

Oven mitts

Plastic zip-top bag

Scissors

Small paper plate

Hole punch

Stretchy bead cording

In a microwave-safe bowl, prepare the candy melts according to the package directions until they are smooth and runny. Remove from the microwave with oven mitts—the bowl will be hot!

Pour the melted candy in a zip-top bag and cut the corner out to make a piping bag. Circle the opening of the cone with the melted candy and place the cone onto the paper plate to secure it in place.

Decorate your party hat using the melted candy and sprinkles.

When done, poke small holes through the sides of the plate and string the cording through the holes to create a chin strap for your hat.

DID YOU KNOW?

Taxis in London are required to be tall enough that a man can sit inside while wearing a bowler hat.

FLOWER CUPCAKE BOUQUET

These flowers are more than just a pretty decoration—they're a yummy treat, too! Build a bouquet of delicious cupcake flowers for a unique gift or a party centerpiece. It is super fun and easy to assemble, and even more fun to eat when you're all done!

ADULT SUPERVISION REQUIRED

MODERATELY HARD

INGREDIENTS

12 yellow candy melts

Yellow nonpareils

1 (1-lb [455-g]) can vanilla frosting

Food coloring

12 unfrosted cupcakes

EQUIPMENT

Oven

Baking sheet

Parchment paper

Oven mitts

Spoon

Bowl

Frosting bag

Styrofoam ball

Flowerpot

Toothpicks

Scissors

Green tissue paper

Preheat the oven to 200°F (100°C). Line a baking sheet with parchment paper.

Place the candy melts onto the lined baking sheet and bake for 2 to 3 minutes. Remove from the oven with oven mitts. Sprinkle the nonpareils on top and allow to harden.

Spoon the frosting into a bowl, add food coloring as desired and then mix thoroughly. Spoon the colored frosting into the icing bag and add frosting petals to the cupcakes. Press one of the candy melts into the center.

Put the Styrofoam ball into the flowerpot and press toothpicks into it. Add the cupcakes to the toothpicks to hold them in place. Cut the green tissue paper into squares and press between the cupcakes.

DID YOU KNOW?
The world record for most cupcakes eaten in the shortest amount of time is 29 cupcakes in 30 seconds.

ADULT SUPERVISION REQUIRED

MODERATE

STAINED GLASS LOLLIPOPS

Have you ever seen a stained glass window in an old building? The sun shines through the colors and makes beautiful patterns. We are going to use that technique to create one-of-a-kind lollipops that are as yummy as they are unique. These stained glass lollipops are translucent, so you can see light shining through. Super fun, right?

INGREDIENTS

18 pieces of colorful hard candy, such as Jolly Ranchers

EQUIPMENT

Oven

Sharp knife

Lollipop mold

Baking sheet

Oven mitts

6 lollipop sticks

Preheat the oven to 275°F (140°C).

Unwrap the candies and separate by color. Get a grown-up to help you cut each candy into pieces with a sharp knife.

Drop the pieces into the cavities of the lollipop mold, combining colors to create patterns. Place the mold on a baking sheet.

Bake for 8 to 10 minutes, until the candies have melted. Remove the baking sheet from the oven with oven mitts. Add a lollipop stick to each mold and turn it to coat the stick with candy.

Allow to harden, then remove from the mold.

DID YOU KNOW?
Tootsie Roll Industries is the world's largest manufacturer of lollipops, turning out 16 million lollipops per day.

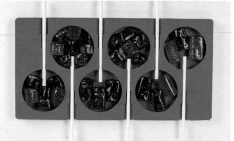 

ADULT SUPERVISION
REQUIRED

MODERATELY HARD

PARTY BANNER

Celebrate good times—and tell everyone about it—with a special party banner that you can EAT! Use our edible dough to build a banner to welcome guests to your party in a way they'll be talking about all night long.

INGREDIENTS

FOR EACH COLOR,
YOU WILL NEED

1 (3-oz [85-g])
package gelatin

¼ cup (60 ml) clear soda

5–6 cups (600–720 g)
confectioners' sugar,
divided

EQUIPMENT

Microwave-safe bowl

Spoon

Microwave

Stand mixer

Rolling pin

Sharp knife

Alphabet fondant
cutters

Straw

String

Combine the gelatin and soda in a microwave-safe bowl and heat for 30 to 40 seconds until completely dissolved. Place in the bowl of a stand mixer.

Add 2 cups (240 g) of the confectioners' sugar to the mixing bowl and mix on low speed until combined. Continue adding confectioners' sugar, ½ cup (60 g) at a time, until a soft dough forms.

Roll out the dough on a clean surface coated with confectioners' sugar. Knead until it is no longer sticky.

Use the knife to cut the pendants for the banner. Cut the letters from a different color of dough. Lightly spread warm water over the back of each letter and attach to a pendant.

Poke a hole in each corner of the pendants with the straw.

Let dry for 24 to 48 hours, then run the string through the holes.

DID YOU KNOW?
August is the most common month for birthdays.

At the Zoo

Lions, tigers and bears, oh my! As a child, my favorite place to visit was the zoo. I loved seeing and learning about all the exotic animals there. Now, you can bring the zoo home with some wild edible crafts.

In this chapter, our edible creations feature some of our favorite zoo animals— from fish in the sea to giant pandas and their lunch. You'll find flamingos, penguins, giraffes and monkeys.

It's a jungle out there!

PANDA COOKIES WITH BAMBOO STICKS

You don't have to head to the zoo to see our favorite black and white critters. With a few ingredients and some crafting skills, you can make your own panda cookies chomping on bamboo sticks.

INGREDIENTS

1 cup (80 g) white candy melts

6 chocolate sandwich cookies, such as Oreos

18 mini chocolate sandwich cookies

12 candy eyes

6 pieces black candy melts

2 pieces green sheet candy, such as Airheads

1 cup (80 g) green candy melts

2 pretzel rods

EQUIPMENT

Microwave-safe bowl

Microwave

Oven mitts

Wax paper

Sharp knife

Food marker

HOW TO MAKE PANDA COOKIES

In a microwave-safe bowl, prepare the white candy melts according to the package directions until they are smooth and runny. Remove from the microwave with oven mitts—the bowl will be hot! Dip a sandwich cookie into the bowl and coat it completely. Remove from the bowl and shake off the excess candy. Place on a sheet of wax paper. This will be your panda's face.

Separate a mini sandwich cookie and remove the middle cream. Place each side onto the coated cookie for the eye patches.

Dip the ends of 2 mini sandwich cookies into the melted white candy and place them as ears onto the top of the bear's face.

Add a dot of melted white candy onto the back of 2 candy eyes and place on top of the eye patches.

With a sharp knife, cut a black candy melt into a triangle and place it under the eyes for the nose. Get an adult to help with this part! Once the candy has hardened, draw a mouth onto your panda's face with the food marker.

HOW TO MAKE BAMBOO STICKS

Use the knife to cut triangles from the green sheet candy. Get an adult to help with this part! Fold the flat end of the triangle to create the end of a leaf shape. Press the edges to mold the candy to look like a leaf.

In a microwave-safe bowl, prepare the green candy melts according to the package directions until they are smooth and runny. Remove from the microwave with oven mitts—the bowl will be hot! Spoon the melted candy onto a pretzel rod to coat it, leaving one end uncovered. Place on wax paper.

Press the leaves onto the melted candy and allow to harden to secure in place.

ZEBRA PRETZEL RODS

It's time to earn your stripes (and make a few treats, too) by creating zebra pretzel rods. Build a herd of these fun animals and pretend to be a zookeeper caring for them. How would you run the zoo if you were in charge?

INGREDIENTS

1 cup (80 g) white candy melts

½ cup (40 g) black candy melts

Pretzel rods

6 candy eyes

3 chocolate chips

3 pieces black licorice laces

EQUIPMENT

3 microwave-safe bowls

Microwave

Oven mitts

Plastic zip-top bag

Scissors

Knife

Set aside a few white candy melts. In microwave-safe bowls, prepare each of the remaining candy melts according to the package directions until they are smooth and runny. Remove from the microwave with oven mitts—the bowl will be hot! Dip a pretzel rod into the melted white candy, coating it fully.

Pour the melted black candy into a plastic zip-top bag and cut off the corner. Add black stripes diagonally across the pretzel stick. Allow to harden.

Cut the reserved white candy melts into triangles and attach to the top of the pretzel rod using melted candy to make ears. Place the candy eyes using melted white candy. Add the chocolate chip for the nose.

Cut the licorice laces to create a mane for the zebra. Dip in the melted white candy and attach to the back of the pretzel rods.

DID YOU KNOW?

Every zebra has a unique pattern of black and white stripes.

LION MARSHMALLOW PIE

MODERATE

This lion just can't wait to be king. Imagine you're the king of the pridelands as you build your lion dessert. What are some challenges a lion might face each day? How do you think they hunt for their food?

INGREDIENTS

¼ cup (20 g) yellow candy melts

Mini marshmallows

1 banana marshmallow pie

Yellow food coloring

Red food coloring

3 tbsp (45 ml) milk

2 candy eyes

EQUIPMENT

Microwave-safe bowl

Microwave

Oven mitts

Bowl

Spoon

Paint brush

Black edible marker

Set aside 2 yellow candy melts. In a microwave-safe bowl, prepare the remaining candy melts according to the package directions until they are smooth and runny. Remove from the microwave with oven mitts—the bowl will be hot! Dip each marshmallow into the melted yellow candy and press onto the outer edge of the marshmallow pie. Place the 2 reserved candy melts using melted candy to create ears.

In a bowl, stir 2 drops of yellow food coloring and 2 drops of red food coloring into the milk to create orange paint. With a paintbrush, coat the outside of the mini marshmallows with the orange paint and allow to dry completely. This will be the lion's mane.

Attach the candy eyes using melted candy. Draw a face on your lion with the edible marker.

DID YOU KNOW?
A lion's roar can be heard up to 5 miles (8 km) away.

MODERATE

GIRAFFE TWINKIES

Let's turn a Twinkie into the tallest animal in the zoo. You'll reach new heights with this creative dessert. So grab your zookeeper hat and let's make a giraffe!

INGREDIENTS

¼ cup (20 g) brown candy melts

Long yellow snack cake, such as a Twinkie

2 yellow candy melts

2 candy eyes

1 mini pretzel stick

EQUIPMENT

Microwave-safe bowl

Microwave

Oven mitts

Plastic zip-top bag

Scissors

Knife

In a microwave-safe bowl, prepare the brown candy melts according to the package directions until they are smooth and runny. Remove from the microwave with oven mitts—the bowl will be hot! Add the brown candy to a zip-top bag and cut the corner out to create a piping bag. Create spots on the snack cake.

Using melted candy, attach a yellow candy melt to the front of the Twinkie for the giraffe's snout. Add the eyes, too.

Break a pretzel stick in half, then coat it in melted brown candy and press into the top of the Twinkie to make antlers.

Cut the remaining yellow candy melt in half and press into the top to make ears.

DID YOU KNOW?
Giraffes can drink 10 gallons (39 L) of water at a time.

TIGER QUESADILLAS

This jungle cat makes the perfect lunch project. Quesadillas are one of my favorite meals to cook. I like them because they are simple to make. My son likes them because they're yummy. Add in tiger stripes and you have a complete winner all around.

ADULT SUPERVISION
REQUIRED

MODERATELY EASY

INGREDIENTS

2 tortillas

3 slices cheddar cheese

1 slice Monterey Jack cheese (or any other white cheese you like!)

EQUIPMENT

Circle cookie cutters in varying sizes

Small skillet

Stove

Black edible marker

Cut the tortillas and a slice of cheddar cheese into large circles using your largest cookie cutter. Place the cut slice of cheddar cheese between 2 tortilla circles and heat in a skillet until the cheese is melted.

Cut a smaller circle from the cheddar cheese and place on top of the quesadilla and allow to cool. Once cool, place a small circle of Monterey Jack cheese to make a snout for your tiger. Add smaller white cheese circles for eyes and smaller cheddar cheese circles for the ears.

Use the black edible marker to draw stripes on the cheddar cheese. Add a nose and mouth to the snout and color in the eyes.

DID YOU KNOW?
Tigers are the largest wild cats in the world.

EDIBLE AQUARIUM

There are plenty of fish in the sea. So why not make your own aquarium? The best part is that you don't have to feed these fish. They'll feed you instead!

ADULT SUPERVISION REQUIRED

MODERATE

INGREDIENTS

1 (3-oz [85-g]) package blue gelatin

¼ cup (20 g) candy crystals, such as Nerds

3 gummy fish

EQUIPMENT

Glass jar with a wide mouth

Knife

Spoon

Bamboo skewer

Prepare the gelatin in a glass jar according to the package directions. Allow to set. Run a knife around the edges of the gelatin and tip upside down to remove it from the container.

Spread candy crystals into the bottom of your jar and replace the gelatin back on top of it. Cut slits into the gelatin and press the candy fish into the slots using the skewer.

DID YOU KNOW?

Fish are one of the oldest animal families. They lived on Earth before dinosaurs.

PENGUIN BANANAS

These penguin bananas are even better frozen—just like penguins in real life, I'd imagine. Make as a yummy treat for yourself or your friends.

ADULT SUPERVISION REQUIRED

MODERATELY EASY

INGREDIENTS

1 cup (80 g) black candy melts

3 bananas

3 orange candy-coated chocolate drops, such as M&M's

6 candy eyes

6 orange candy melt wafers

2 large square marshmallows

EQUIPMENT

Microwave-safe bowl

Microwave

Oven mitts

Knife

Wax paper

In a microwave-safe bowl, prepare the candy melts according to the package directions until they are smooth and runny. Remove from the microwave with oven mitts—the bowl will be hot!

Peel the bananas and cut them in half. Dip the bananas in the candy melts to coat them. Place on wax paper.

Press the orange chocolate drops onto the chocolate to make a beak and add the candy eyes. Add 2 orange candy melt wafers to the bottom of the bananas to make feet. Cut the square marshmallows in half and place on the bananas sticky-side down to make the penguins' bellies. Chill until hard.

DID YOU KNOW?
Penguin feathers trap a layer of warm air next to their skin to keep them warm.

NO ADULT SUPERVISION
REQUIRED

●○○○○

EASY

POLAR BEAR SANDWICHES

Catch an ice floe and enjoy a meal fit for a polar bear. A super exciting way to spice up mealtime is to turn a sandwich into something fun. Polar bears are a great choice because you can use white bread for their fur and face. So easy!

INGREDIENTS

2 pieces white sandwich bread

1 slice sandwich meat/cheese

3 olive slices

EQUIPMENT

Circle cookie cutters in varying sizes

Prepare your sandwich with the bread and meat and/or cheese, then cut out the polar bear's face with a large circle cookie cutter. Cut ears using a smaller circle cookie cutter. Cut another small circle for the snout.

Add olive slices for the eyes and nose.

DID YOU KNOW?

A polar bear's fur isn't actually white! It's transparent and reflects sunlight to help the polar bear blend into its snowy surroundings.

MODERATE

MONKEY SANDWICHES

Here's another fun animal sandwich idea.

I'm not monkeying around—these monkey sandwiches are so much fun to make! Your friends will be swinging from the trees when they see just how awesome your lunch is.

INGREDIENTS

3 tbsp (45 g) peanut butter

3 pieces wheat bread

1 piece white bread

2 candy eyes

1 tbsp (15 g) chocolate-hazelnut spread, such as Nutella

EQUIPMENT

Butter knife

Circle cookie cutters in varying sizes

Sharp knife

Plastic zip-top bag

Scissors

With a butter knife, spread some of the peanut butter between 2 slices of wheat bread, then cut the sandwich into a circle using a large cookie cutter.

Cut a piece of white bread using the same cookie cutter, but ask a grown-up to use the sharp knife to round it into more of an oval shape, creating a snout for the monkey. Attach the white bread with peanut butter.

Cut 2 smaller circles from the wheat bread and use peanut butter to place them as the monkey's ears. Spread peanut butter on the monkey's face to place the candy eyes.

Add the chocolate-hazelnut spread to the zip-top bag and cut off the corner to use as a piping bag. Draw a mouth and nostrils on the monkey's face. Add some dollops of chocolate spread on the monkey's ears.

GET CREATIVE!

Substitute raisins, grapes, sliced bananas or other fruit to decorate the monkey's face.

DID YOU KNOW?

Monkeys peel the skin from the bananas they eat!

FLAMINGO MARSHMALLOW POPS

Flamingos are just such a cool animal, why wouldn't you want to make your own? This one is made from cookies and marshmallows, which makes it that much better.

ADULT SUPERVISION REQUIRED

MODERATE

INGREDIENTS

1 cup (80 g) pink candy melts

¼ cup (20 g) black candy melts

1 tbsp (5 g) orange candy melts

3 jumbo marshmallows

6 strawberry wafer cookies

EQUIPMENT

3 microwave-safe bowls

Microwave

Oven mitts

Knife

Wax paper

In microwave-safe bowls, prepare each of the candy melts according to the package directions until they are smooth and runny. Remove from the microwave with oven mitts—the bowls will be hot! Coat a jumbo marshmallow in the melted pink candy.

Cut a strawberry wafer cookie in half lengthwise. Place into the bottom of the marshmallow for legs. Cut another wafer cookie into pieces to create the flamingo's neck, the longer piece, and head, the shorter piece.

Dip the ends of the shorter wafer cookie in the melted black candy, then in the melted orange candy to make a beak. Attach the pieces with melted pink candy.

Place on wax paper and allow to harden completely.

DID YOU KNOW?

Flamingos get their pink color from the crustaceans and plankton they eat.

On the Farm

Now let's head to the farm to visit some more of our favorite animals. Farm life can be rough, with all the hay and dirt and work. So why not bring the farm inside with some yummy treats?

This chapter features all the animals you'd find on a farm—ducks, chickens, horses and pigs, plus a few surprises thrown in. A pumpkin patch? And some mud that you can eat? Sounds like a down-home good time to me.

EASY

PIGGY PANCAKES

Breakfast is the most important meal of the day, so let's enjoy a pigtastic one with no bacon in sight. It's the perfect meal for a farmer in training!

INGREDIENTS

3 pancakes

¼ cup (60 g) chocolate-hazelnut spread, such as Nutella

1 tbsp (11 g) chocolate chips

EQUIPMENT

Circle cookie cutters

Butter knife

Plastic zip-top bag

Scissors

Place one pancake down for the body. Cut a smaller circle from a second pancake for the head of your piggy and use a butter knife to spread chocolate-hazelnut spread on the bottom. Place it on top of the body.

Cut a smaller circle from a pancake for the snout. Spread chocolate-hazelnut spread on the bottom and put it in place. Press 2 chocolate chips onto the snout. Add 2 more for the eyes.

Cut 2 triangles from pancakes for the ears and place on top of the head. Attach with chocolate-hazelnut spread.

Put some chocolate-hazelnut spread in the zip-top bag and cut the corner to make a piping bag. Swirl the chocolate-hazelnut spread on the back of the body to make a tail.

DID YOU KNOW?

Mother pigs, called sows, have been known to sing to their piglets.

EDIBLE MUD

EASY

Do you remember making mud pies as a little kid? Well, now you can make mud pies that are actually edible. So tell Mom not to worry, you've got this.

Place the cookies in a plastic zip-top bag and crush with the rolling pin.

Add some of the cookie crumbs in the bottom of a plastic cup. Add the chocolate pudding, then layer more cookie crumbles on top.

Put gummy worms into the edible mud for a fun treat.

INGREDIENTS

12 chocolate sandwich cookies, such as Oreos

3 cups (850 g) chocolate pudding

9 gummy worms

EQUIPMENT

Plastic zip-top bag

Rolling pin

3 plastic cups

DID YOU KNOW?
A worm has no eyes.

ADULT SUPERVISION
REQUIRED

MODERATELY EASY

HORSE GRAHAM CRACKERS

Saddle up for a project that will knock your boots off. We're going to turn graham crackers into a horse-themed snack that will make any ranch hand jealous. Every good farmer has a trusty horse.

INGREDIENTS

¾ cup (180 g)
chocolate-hazelnut
spread, such as Nutella

6 graham crackers

3 peanut butter candy
melts

12 candy eyes

12 mini chocolate chips

EQUIPMENT

Sharp knife

Spread chocolate-hazelnut spread on the graham crackers. Have a grown-up cut a peanut butter candy melt in quarters and press onto the top of the cracker for ears.

Place 2 candy eyes, then add 2 chocolate chips to the bottom of the cracker for a snout.

DID YOU KNOW?
Horses have bigger eyes than any other land mammal.

SHEEP DOUGHNUTS

No need to shear, sheep doughnuts are here! And we're going to make them. No farm is complete without some sheep in the pasture. Powdered doughnuts are soft and fluffy and the perfect base for our sheep.

INGREDIENTS

¼ cup (20 g) peanut butter candy melts

6 powdered doughnuts

12 candy eyes

6 pink heart sprinkles

EQUIPMENT

Microwave-safe bowl

Microwave

Oven mitts

Sharp knife

Set aside 12 peanut butter candy melt wafers. In a microwave-safe bowl, prepare a small amount of the candy melts according to the package directions until they are smooth and runny. Remove from the microwave with oven mitts—the bowl will be hot! This will be your glue for your creation.

Adhere an unmelted candy wafer in the middle of a doughnut, smooth side facing out, for the sheep's face. Have a grown-up cut another unmelted candy wafer in half and adhere in place with the melted candy for the ears. Add the candy eyes and a heart sprinkle upside down for the nose.

DID YOU KNOW?
There are more than 1 billion sheep in the world.

MODERATELY EASY

EDIBLE DUCK POND

Duck, duck, goose. Or really just duck, duck, duck. Head on down to the duck pond with this fun project. What else could you find in a duck pond?

INGREDIENTS

1 (6-oz [170-g]) package blue gelatin

3 jumbo marshmallows

3 mini marshmallows

1 cup (80 g) yellow candy melts

6 mini orange candy-coated chocolate drops, such as M&M's

EQUIPMENT

Heatproof bowl

Spoon

6 plastic cups

Sharp knife

Microwave-safe bowl

Microwave

Oven mitts

Black edible marker

Prepare the gelatin in a heatproof bowl according to the package directions. Pour into 6 small cups. Allow to set.

Have a grown-up cut a jumbo marshmallow and a mini marshmallow in half. In a microwave-safe bowl, prepare the candy melts according to the package directions until they are smooth and runny. Remove from the microwave with oven mitts—the bowl will be hot! Coat the marshmallow halves in the melted candy. Add the mini chocolate drops to the small marshmallows for a beak and place on the large marshmallows. Use the marker to add dots for the duck's eyes.

Place on top of the gelatin so it looks like the ducks are floating in the pond!

DID YOU KNOW?
Ducks can be found on every continent except Antarctica.

NO ADULT SUPERVISION REQUIRED

MODERATE

CHICKEN COOP

Which came first, the chicken or the chicken coop? You get to decide. And when you're done building the coop and making the chickens, don't forget to collect their eggs.

In microwave-safe bowls, prepare each of the candy melts according to the package directions until they are smooth and runny. Remove from the microwave with oven mitts—the bowl will be hot!

Coat the pretzel twists in the melted yellow candy and place on wax paper to harden. Place candy eyes and orange chocolate drops for a beak.

Dip the end of a pretzel stick in the melted chocolate candy and place on the wax paper. Use the pretzel sticks to build a fence by connecting 2 sticks horizontally with another one vertically.

Place the chicks inside the fence.

INGREDIENTS

¼ cup (20 g) yellow candy melts

¼ cup (20 g) light cocoa candy melts

3 mini pretzel twists

6 candy eyes

3 mini orange candy-coated chocolate drops, such as M&M's

16 pretzel sticks

EQUIPMENT

2 microwave-safe bowls

Microwave

Oven mitts

Wax paper

DID YOU KNOW?
Chickens are related to the Tyrannosaurus Rex.

MODERATE

KITTY CAT TORTILLA SNACK

This snack is utterly purrrrrfect. Cats do everything from catch mice to keep humans company on a farm. Where would your kitty spend its days?

INGREDIENTS

1 tbsp (15 g) cream cheese

1 tbsp (15 g) strawberry jelly

2 wheat tortillas

1 tbsp (15 g) chocolate-hazlenut spread, such as Nutella

2 candy eyes

EQUIPMENT

Butter knife

Circle cookie cutter

Plastic zip-top bag

Scissors

With a butter knife, spread the cream cheese and jelly on a tortilla. Place the other tortilla on top and use the cookie cutter to cut the snack into a smaller circle.

Cut triangle-shaped ears from the leftover end piece.

Put some chocolate-hazelnut spread in the plastic zip-top bag and cut the corner to make a piping bag. Use it to attach the ears to the top of the circle cutout. Put a dollop of chocolate-hazelnut spread on the back of each candy eye and place on the front of the circle. Draw a nose and whiskers using the chocolate-hazelnut spread beneath the eyes.

DID YOU KNOW?
Cats can sleep 13 to 14 hours a day.

PUPPY PEANUT BUTTER CUPS

Have you ever wanted a puppy? Well, let's make one! Pretend your puppy is a ranch dog that is responsible for watching over the farm's livestock. Does it like to chase chickens? Herd cattle? After a long day on the farm, it's time for a nice meal and yummy dessert. So eat up!

INGREDIENTS

12 pieces chocolate-flavored taffy roll, such as Tootsie Rolls

¼ cup (20 g) black candy melts

4 peanut butter cups

8 candy eyes

EQUIPMENT

Microwave-safe bowl

Microwave

Oven mitts

Plastic zip-top bag

Scissors

Unwrap the taffy rolls and knead with your fingers to shape into puppy ears. Tear off a small piece and roll into a nose. Tear off another piece and flatten into a circle. Make enough for 4 puppies.

In a microwave-safe bowl, prepare the candy melts according to the package directions until they are smooth and runny. Remove from the microwave with oven mitts—the bowl will be hot! Add to the plastic zip-top bag and cut out the corner to make a piping bag. Use the melted candy as glue to attach the puppy ears, nose and flat circle as a patch for one of the puppy's eyes. Add the puppy's eyes.

DID YOU KNOW?
The most popular dog in the world is the Labrador. It has the most registered owners worldwide.

PUMPKIN PATCH

It's harvest time! Grab your garden tools and let's get to crafting an awesome pumpkin patch. Tending the garden is one of a farmer's most important jobs, so let's pretend we are gathering pumpkins for a fall celebration. What other crops could a farmer grow?

ADULT SUPERVISION
RECOMMENDED

MODERATELY HARD

INGREDIENTS

12 chocolate sandwich cookies, such as Oreos

¼ cup (20 g) white candy melts

8 vanilla wafer cookies

4 pumpkin candies

¼ cup (20 g) green candy melts

EQUIPMENT

3 plastic zip-top bags

Rolling pin

2 microwave-safe bowls

Microwave

Oven mitts

Scissors

Wax paper

Knife

Place the sandwich cookies in a plastic zip-top bag and crush with the rolling pin. Set aside.

In a microwave-safe bowl, prepare the white candy melts according to the package directions until they are smooth and runny. Remove from the microwave with oven mitts—the bowl will be hot! Pour into a plastic bag and snip the corner to make a piping bag. Lay out 4 vanilla wafer cookies on the wax paper side by side. Glue together by running a line of melted white candy down the sides and pressing together.

Cut 2 vanilla wafer cookies to the width of the block you just made and put in place as the sides of a fence using the melted white candy. Add another 2 cookies horizontally using the melted candy to create the other sides.

Fill your fence with the crushed cookies and add some pumpkins to the "dirt."

In a microwave-safe bowl, prepare the green candy melts, remove from the microwave with oven mitts and put in a zip-top bag. Snip the corner for a piping bag and draw vines coming from the pumpkins.

DID YOU KNOW?

Some pumpkins have been known to weigh more than 1,000 pounds (454 kg).

out in space

When you look into the night sky, do you picture the planets so far away? Do you see the stars and dream of the constellations they create?

Then this chapter is for you. I've imagined some projects for you that are so big, they're out of this world. So have a pizza planet for dinner and a chocolate rocket ship for dessert. The galaxy is out there waiting.

PIZZA PLANETS

Build a model of the solar system entirely out of pizza or just make one or two of your favorite planets. And then have a delicious dinner when it's all over.

HARD

INGREDIENTS

1 (1-lb [454-g]) package refrigerated pizza dough

All-purpose flour, for rolling

2 cups (470 ml) pizza sauce

1 cup (120 g) shredded mozzarella cheese

Pizza toppings (like pepperoni and olives)

EQUIPMENT

Oven

Baking sheet

Parchment paper

Rolling pin

Cookie cutters

Pizza cutter

Oven mitts

Preheat the oven to 400°F (200°C). Line a baking sheet with parchment paper.

With a rolling pin, roll out the pizza dough on a lightly floured surface and cut out circles using the cookie cutters. You'll need one circle for each pizza you are making.

Use the pizza cutter to slice strips of dough from the leftover pieces and lay the dough across the circle to make a ring around your planet.

Spread pizza sauce on the dough and sprinkle cheese on top. Decorate the rest of your pizza planet with your desired pizza toppings. Place on the prepared baking sheet.

Bake for 8 to 10 minutes, or until the crust is golden brown. Have a grown-up remove the baking sheet from the oven with oven mitts and let the pizza cool a bit before enjoying.

DID YOU KNOW?

Earth has more exposed water than land—three-fourths of the Earth is covered in water!

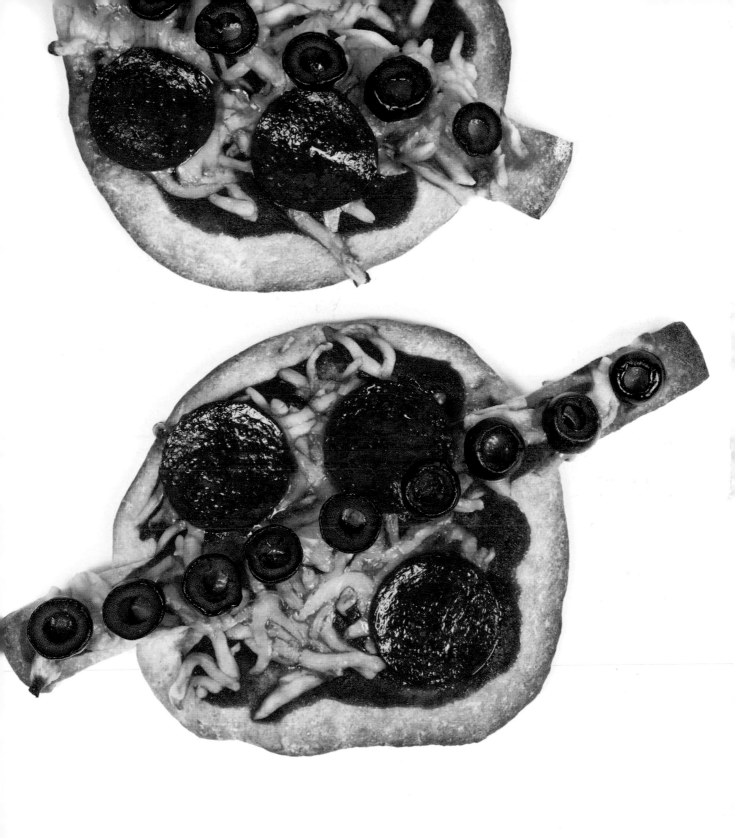

ADULT SUPERVISION
RECOMMENDED

MODERATELY EASY

CHOCOLATE ROCKET SHIP

Fly to the moon and back with a chocolate rocket ship built for a trip to the stars. If you could travel anywhere in space, where would you go?

INGREDIENTS

¼ cup (20 g) dark chocolate candy melts

¼ cup (20 g) white candy melts

1 snack-size chocolate cake roll, such as Ho Ho

3 chocolate kisses, such as Hershey's

4 pieces orange and red sheet candy, such as Airheads

EQUIPMENT

2 microwave-safe bowls

Microwave

Oven mitts

Plastic zip-top bag

Scissors

Spoon or butter knife

Sharp knife

In microwave-safe bowls, prepare the candy melts according to the package directions until they are smooth and runny. Remove from the microwave with oven mitts—the bowl will be hot!

Add the white candy melts to a zip-top bag and cut a corner to make a piping bag. Write USA down the middle of the chocolate cake.

Spread the melted chocolate onto the flat portion of a chocolate kiss and place on the end of the chocolate cake roll. Add 2 kisses to the other end for the bottom of the rocket.

Flatten the orange and red sheet candy and cut into the shape of flames. Place beneath the rocket to show it lifting off!

DID YOU KNOW?
Yuri Gagarin, the first human to enter outer space, traveled there by rocket.

ADULT SUPERVISION
REQUIRED

MODERATELY EASY

GLOWING GELATIN ALIENS

Let's pretend we're at Area 51 and just uncovered an alien spacecraft. You check inside and find glowing aliens. What do you do?

No, these gelatin aliens didn't undergo some crazy science experiment. They are just so awesome that they glow. And you're so awesome you can eat them.

INGREDIENTS

1 (6-oz [170-g]) package lime gelatin

2 cups (470 ml) cold tonic water

EQUIPMENT

Bowl

Spoon

Alien mold

Baking sheet

Cookie cutter or knife

Black light

Mix the gelatin and tonic water in a bowl. Stir for 2 minutes until it's completely dissolved.

Pour into the alien mold and chill for 4 hours, or until firm.

You can also pour the mixture onto a baking sheet and chill, then cut out alien shapes with a cookie cutter or knife.

Serve under a black light for a glowing treat!

DID YOU KNOW?

The word *alien* means "stranger." It comes from Latin and means "strange" or "foreign."

GALAXY BARK

Swirl the colors of the galaxy together to create a space-worthy masterpiece that is as delicious as it is beautiful. Add in a mishmash of sprinkles, glitter dust and other pieces to make a galaxy effect that resembles all the unique textures you can find in space.

ADULT SUPERVISION REQUIRED

MODERATELY EASY

INGREDIENTS

1 cup (80 g) black candy melts

1 cup (80 g) white candy melts

1 cup (80 g) purple candy melts

1 cup (80 g) blue candy melts

4 tbsp (40 g) star sprinkles

2 tsp (2 g) edible glitter dust

EQUIPMENT

Baking sheet

Wax paper

4 microwave-safe bowls

Microwave

Oven mitts

Spoon

Line a baking sheet with wax paper. In microwave-safe bowls, prepare each of the candy melts according to the package directions until they are smooth and runny. Remove from the microwave with oven mitts—the bowls will be hot! Spoon onto the wax paper, randomly placing the colors. Use a spoon to swirl the colors together to give the appearance of the galaxy. Add star sprinkles and edible glitter dust to finish it off.

GET CREATIVE!
Use other colors to make edible candy bark—blue and green could make Earth bark; red, yellow and orange for sun bark. Are there any other planets you could create?

DID YOU KNOW?
The high and low tides on Earth are caused by the gravitational pulls of the sun and moon.

ADULT SUPERVISION
REQUIRED

MODERATE

STAINED GLASS STARS

These cool cookies are out of this world! Hold them up to a lamp and watch as the light shines through. Imagine you just encountered a falling star. What would you wish for?

INGREDIENTS

4 cups (960 g) Sugar Cookie Dough (page 15)

¼ cup (20 g) hard colorful candies, such as Jolly Ranchers

EQUIPMENT

Oven

Baking sheet

Parchment paper

Rolling pin

Star cookie cutters (2 sizes)

Plastic zip-top bag

Oven mitts

Preheat the oven to 350°F (180°C). Line a baking sheet with parchment paper.

On a clean surface, roll out the sugar cookie dough with a rolling pin. Use the larger star cookie cutter to make star cookies. Cut a smaller star from the center of each cookie and remove the extra dough to leave an opening. Place on the prepared baking sheet.

Unwrap the candies and place in a zip-top bag. Crush with the rolling pin.

Sprinkle the candy pieces in the center opening of each cookie.

Have a grown-up transfer the baking sheet to the oven and bake for 8 to 10 minutes, until the cookies are light brown. Have a grown-up remove the baking sheet with oven mitts and allow the cookies to cool completely before serving.

The candy will have melted in the oven and filled the empty star in each cookie. As it cools, the candy will harden and create a stained glass look in each star.

GET CREATIVE!
Hold your star cookies up to the light and see what happens. Can you see through the stained glass?

DID YOU KNOW?
Even though our sun looks big to us, it's considered just a medium-size star.

NO ADULT SUPERVISION
REQUIRED

MODERATELY EASY

CONSTELLATION GRAHAM CRACKERS

Learn about the night sky with these fun snacks, then design your own constellations for a new twist. What would you name your constellation?

INGREDIENTS

1 cup (80 g) black candy melts

6 graham crackers

2 tbsp (20 g) gold star sprinkles

1 (7-oz [196-g]) package white cookie icing

Edible gold dust

EQUIPMENT

Microwave-safe bowl

Microwave

Oven mitts

Butter knife

In a microwave-safe bowl, prepare the candy melts according to the package directions until they are smooth and runny. Remove from the microwave with oven mitts—the bowl will be hot!

Break a graham cracker in half and use the butter knife to spread the melted candy melts onto the front of one half.

Place the star sprinkles onto the melted chocolate and allow to harden. Connect the stars with the cookie icing and sprinkle gold dust onto the connecting lines.

Allow to dry completely before serving.

GET CREATIVE!
Find a picture of a well-known constellation and see if you can copy it onto your crackers. Now make your own! What shape would your constellation be if you could create one?

DID YOU KNOW?
Orion is one of the most visible constellations. It can be seen throughout the world.

For the Holidays

From Valentine's Day to Christmas, holidays provide great themes for some fun, edible crafts. These dates give us a reason to pause and think, to stop and create.

This chapter puts a twist on traditional holiday crafts. If you want to build a snowman, grab a bag of pretzels. Make a monster with edible vampire teeth. Turn a doughnut into a pumpkin. Whether you're making these crafts for a class party or just because, you'll find something for every occasion.

STRAWBERRY SANTAS AND CHRISTMAS TREES

Ho, ho, ho! Santa may love cookies, but these strawberry treats are a close second. Build a winter scene with these Strawberry Santas and Christmas Trees. They'll look great on a party table or as a yummy snack.

MODERATE

INGREDIENTS

12 strawberries

1 cup (240 g) vanilla frosting

12 candy eyes

6 mini marshmallows

1 cup (80 g) green candy melts

2 tbsp (20 g) white nonpareils

6 star sprinkles

EQUIPMENT

Knife

Spoon

Plastic zip-top bags

Scissors

Wax paper

Microwave-safe bowl

Microwave

Oven mitts

Remove the stems from the strawberries. Ask a grown-up to help cut the point off 6 strawberries to make Santa's hats.

Spoon some vanilla frosting into a plastic bag, then cut off the corner to make a piping bag. Add vanilla frosting on top of the strawberry to make Santa's face. Pipe some down the front to make a beard. Add candy eyes. Place the tip of the strawberry back on top and add a dollop of white frosting to his hat. Add a mini marshmallow to the frosting.

In a microwave-safe bowl, prepare the candy melts according to the package directions until they are smooth and runny. Remove from the microwave with oven mitts—the bowl will be hot! Cover the remaining 6 strawberries in green candy and tap to remove excess. Set on wax paper and sprinkle with white nonpareils. Add a star sprinkle to the top. Allow to harden.

DID YOU KNOW?

During the seventeenth and eighteenth centuries, some people hung Christmas trees upside down from the ceiling!

MODERATELY EASY

REINDEER COOKIES

These reindeer may not guide Santa's sleigh, but they sure do know the way to a full belly. Make some and pretend you have to guide Santa through a storm on Christmas Eve. How do you make all the deliveries in time? And where would you stop first?

In a microwave-safe bowl, prepare the candy melts according to the package directions until they are smooth and runny. Remove from the microwave with oven mitts—the bowl will be hot! Coat the cookies in the melted candy and place on wax paper to harden. Add the candy eyes and a chocolate drop nose on the front of the cookie.

Break a pretzel twist in half and place at the top of the cookie for antlers.

INGREDIENTS

1 cup (80 g) light cocoa candy melts

5 sandwich cookies, such as Oreos

10 candy eyes

5 candy-coated chocolate drops, such as M&M's

5 pretzel twists

EQUIPMENT

Microwave-safe bowl

Microwave

Oven mitts

Wax paper

DID YOU KNOW?

Santa originally had eight reindeer—Dasher, Dancer, Prancer, Vixen, Comet, Cupid, Donner and Blitzen. His ninth reindeer, Rudolph, was added later.

GRINCH HEART MARSHMALLOW POPS

MODERATELY EASY

How the Grinch Stole Christmas by Dr. Seuss is one of my favorite holiday stories. We read it every year as a family. What are some of your favorite winter stories?

Your heart will grow three sizes when you make this fun project. Promise.

INGREDIENTS

1 cup (80 g) green candy melts

4 jumbo marshmallows

4 heart sprinkles

EQUIPMENT

Microwave-safe bowl

Microwave

Oven mitts

4 lollipop sticks

Styrofoam block

In a microwave-safe bowl, prepare the candy melts according to the package directions until they are smooth and runny. Remove from the microwave with oven mitts—the bowl will be hot! Dip the end of a lollipop stick in the melted candy, then insert into a marshmallow. Coat the marshmallow in the green candy and add a heart sprinkle to the front. Place in the styrofoam block and allow to harden.

GET CREATIVE!
If you can't find heart sprinkles, try drawing a heart with melted red candy or candy markers!

DID YOU KNOW?
The Grinch was originally black and white with pink eyes.

ADULT SUPERVISION REQUIRED

MODERATELY HARD

JOLLY ELF COOKIES

When they aren't busy in the North Pole, elves make great holiday cookies. Let's make some and pretend to be in Santa's workshop getting ready for Christmas. What toy would you be in charge of making?

INGREDIENTS

¼ cup (20 g) peanut butter candy melts, divided

¼ cup (20 g) green candy melts

¼ cup (20 g) red candy melts

4 peanut-shaped sandwich cookies, such as Nutter Butters

8 candy eyes

4 mini marshmallows

2 tbsp (20 g) white nonpareils

EQUIPMENT

3 microwave-safe bowls

Microwave

Oven mitts

Wax paper

Plastic zip-top bag

Scissors

Knife

Set aside 4 peanut butter candy melts. In microwave-safe bowls, prepare each of the candy melts according to the package directions until they are smooth and runny. Remove from the microwave with oven mitts—the bowls will be hot! Dip the top and bottom of 2 of the cookies into the green melted candy, leaving an uncovered section for the elf's face. Place on wax paper to set. Repeat with the remaining 2 cookies and the red melted candy.

Add the melted peanut butter candy to a zip-top bag and cut the corner to make a piping bag. Attach the candy eyes to the elf's face using the melted peanut butter candy. Cut the reserved peanut butter candy melts in half and add them to the sides of the elf's face for ears, and a mini marshmallow at the top of the elf's hat.

Line the top of the elf's shirt and bottom of the elf's hat with melted candy, then sprinkle with white nonpareils.

DID YOU KNOW?

The famous sculptor Michelangelo once built a snowman for an Italian politician.

SNOWMAN PRETZELS

Do you want to build a snowman? Okay, then grab some pretzels and let's make it happen! It doesn't have to be cold outside to make this winter favorite!

INGREDIENTS

¼ cup (20 g) white candy melts

¼ cup (20 g) black candy melts

3 circle pretzels

1 tsp mini candy-coated chocolate drops, such as M&M's

1 tsp mini chocolate chips

1 small orange hard mint, such as a Tic Tac

3 pretzel sticks

1 square pretzel

EQUIPMENT

2 microwave-safe bowls

Microwave

Oven mitts

Wax paper

Spoon

In microwave-safe bowls, prepare each of the candy melts according to the package directions until they are smooth and runny. Remove from the microwave with oven mitts—the bowls will be hot! On the wax paper, lay 3 circle pretzels vertically and spoon melted white candy into the circles, slightly overlapping where they connect so they will stick together.

Add mini chocolate drops for buttons and mini chocolate chips for eyes. A small orange mint makes the nose. Dip 2 pretzel sticks in the melted white candy and attach to the sides as arms.

Place the last pretzel stick across the top of the highest circle, then add the square pretzel. Spoon melted black candy over it to make a top hat.

DID YOU KNOW?
Building a snowman burns more calories than dancing!

FRANKENSTEIN'S MONSTER FRUIT

It's alllliiiivvveee. And it tastes like kiwi. Who knew that a kiwi could turn into the most famous monster ever? Grab a grown-up for this project and get to carving. What other fruits could you turn into monsters?

INGREDIENTS

1 kiwi

2 candy eyes

Black icing

1 mini pretzel stick

EQUIPMENT

Sharp knife

Cut the bottom off the kiwi to make it flat, then cut the sides to make your kiwi have a square shape. Peel most of the kiwi, leaving some skin on the top with a jagged edge to make it look like hair.

Attach candy eyes with the black icing. Draw stitches and a mouth on the face using icing. Break the pretzel stick into smaller pieces and insert them in the sides of the kiwi to make neck bolts.

DID YOU KNOW?

Frankenstein by Mary Shelley is considered one of the first science fiction novels.

MODERATELY EASY

VAMPIRE DOUGHNUTS

"I vant to eat your doughnuts." That's totally what Dracula said, right? Turn plain ol' glazed doughnuts into spooky vampires for a Halloween treat your friends will freak out over.

INGREDIENTS

6 glazed doughnuts

24 pieces candy corn

Black gel icing

12 candy eyes

EQUIPMENT

Wax paper

Place a doughnut on the wax paper and insert 4 candy corn into the center of the doughnut to make teeth.

Use the black gel icing to add hair to your vampire.

Attach the candy eyes under the black hair using some of the gel icing.

GET CREATIVE!

You can use plastic vampire teeth instead of candy corn to give your vampire doughnuts a more realistic look.

DID YOU KNOW?

The most famous vampire is Count Dracula, who is a character in a novel written by Bram Stoker.

NO ADULT SUPERVISION
REQUIRED

MODERATELY EASY

MONSTER APPLE SLICES

Monsters don't have to be scary. They can be yummy, too! And these monster apple slices prove it.

INGREDIENTS

6 apple slices

3 tbsp (45 g) peanut butter

¼ cup (25 g) almond slivers

12 candy eyes

EQUIPMENT

Paper towels

Butter knife

Use paper towels to pat the apple slices dry. Spread peanut butter on one side of each apple slice.

Place 2 apple slices together to make a "V" shape, with the skin of the apple pointing toward you. One slice will be lying flat (peanut butter facing up) and the other will be sitting vertically (with the peanut butter toward you).

Press almond slivers into the apple slices to make teeth. Use peanut butter to attach candy eyes to the top apple slice.

GET CREATIVE!
What other ways can you dress up your monsters? Add pretzel sticks for hair or give them grapes for eyes.

DID YOU KNOW?
Apple trees don't grow apples until they are at least four to five years old!

JACK-O'-LANTERN QUESADILLAS

MODERATELY EASY

This Halloween, carve jack-o'-lantern quesadillas after you're done carving pumpkins. In my family, we have a tradition of making a spooky dinner together before we go trick-or-treating, and this is one of our favorites!

INGREDIENTS

12 tortillas

2 cups (240 g) shredded cheddar cheese

6 slices cheddar cheese

EQUIPMENT

Sharp knife

Skillet

Stove

Ask a grown-up to use a sharp knife to cut a jack-o'-lantern face in 6 of the tortillas. Set aside.

Place a plain tortilla in the skillet and add ⅓ cup (40 g) of shredded cheese on top. Cook over medium-high heat for a few minutes, until the cheese starts to melt. Place the jack-o'-lantern tortilla on top and remove from the heat.

Add a square piece of cheese to the top for a stem.

DID YOU KNOW?
Jack-o'-lanterns were originally carved from turnips, gourds, potatoes and beets.

COLORFUL TURKEY COOKIES

Gobble gobble down this yummy treat that is perfect for the kids' table at your Thanksgiving feast. Make some to share with friends or save them for yourself—these turkeys won't put you in a tryptophan coma at the end of the day.

INGREDIENTS

1 cup (80 g) dark cocoa candy melts

6 peanut-shaped sandwich cookies, such as Nutter Butters

42 pieces candy corn

12 candy eyes

6 pieces red gummy candy

EQUIPMENT

Microwave-safe bowl

Microwave

Oven mitts

Wax paper

Knife

In a microwave-safe bowl, prepare the candy melts according to the package directions until they are smooth and runny. Remove from the microwave with oven mitts—the bowl will be hot!

Dip the cookies into the melted candy and set on wax paper to dry.

Cut the end off a piece of candy corn and attach it for a beak. Add 2 candy eyes and a red gummy candy for the turkey's snood. Add 6 candy corn around the cookie for the turkey's tail feathers. Repeat for each cookie.

DID YOU KNOW?

Turkeys don't have to move their head to see behind them! Their eyes have almost 360 degrees of vision.

● ○ ○ ○ ○

EASY

PUMPKIN DOUGHNUTS

Fall is in the air and that means it's time for pumpkin everything. These doughnuts may not be pumpkin flavored, but they're cute and that's all that matters, right? Whip up a batch to enjoy while carving this year's jack-o'-lantern.

INGREDIENTS

6 powdered doughnuts

Edible orange spray coloring

3 mini pretzel sticks

6 pieces green gummy candy

EQUIPMENT

Parchment paper

Kitchen scissors

Place the doughnuts on parchment paper and spray with the orange food coloring. Break the pretzel sticks in half and insert a stick at the top for the stem. Use scissors to cut a leaf shape out of the green gummy candy and attach it to the pretzel stick.

DID YOU KNOW?
Most pumpkins are orange, but they can also be green, yellow and white.

CUPID'S ARROW BREAKFAST STICKS

This Valentine's Day, Cupid's arrow leads to a yummy breakfast and a full belly. So start your day off right with a healthy meal or make a batch to bring to a Valentine's Day party. You could even make one for your sweetheart and attach a special note.

ADULT SUPERVISION REQUIRED

EASY

INGREDIENTS

6 strawberries

4 cups (120 g) colorful ring-shaped cereal, such as Froot Loops or Cheerios

1 cup (150 g) blueberries

6 orange slices

EQUIPMENT

Sharp knife

Small heart-shaped cookie cutter

6 bamboo skewers

Have a grown-up help you cut a strawberry in half vertically, then use the cookie cutter to cut it into a heart shape. Stick the heart onto the end of the bamboo skewer to make an arrowhead.

Slide the ring cereal onto the skewer, creating patterns or using like-colored cereal together for the body of your arrow.

When you get close to the end, add a few blueberries and then the orange slices to make fletching for your arrow.

Repeat with the other skewers to make a fun Valentine's Day breakfast everyone can enjoy!

DID YOU KNOW?
Teachers receive more cards on Valentine's Day than any other profession.

PEPPERMINT CANDY HEARTS

Delicious and perfect for the holidays, these peppermint candy hearts are as stunning as they are simple. They make the perfect homemade gift for the holidays, or a sweet treat for your sweetheart.

INGREDIENTS

12 small candy canes

1 cup (80 g) white candy melts

Heart sprinkles

EQUIPMENT

Wax paper

Microwave-safe bowl

Microwave

Oven mitts

Spoon

Place 2 candy canes side by side on the wax paper so they make the shape of a heart.

In a microwave-safe bowl, prepare the candy melts according to the package directions until they are smooth and runny. Remove from the microwave with oven mitts—the bowl will be hot!

Spoon the melted candy into the middle of the candy canes. Add a heart sprinkle and allow to harden.

DID YOU KNOW?

Candy canes used to be all white. In the 1900s, the first candy canes with red stripes appeared.

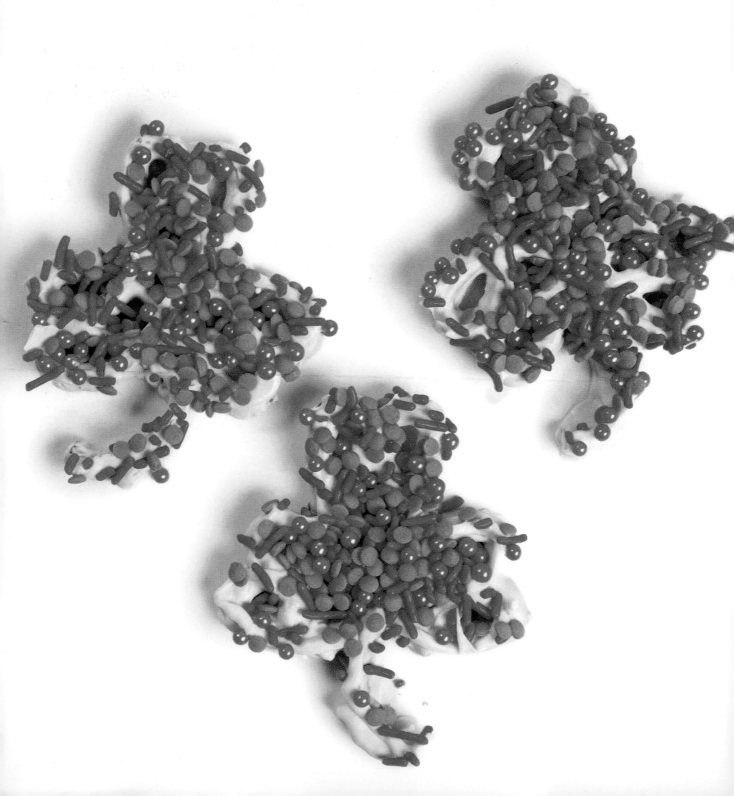

ADULT SUPERVISION
REQUIRED

MODERATELY EASY

INGREDIENTS

1 cup (80 g) white candy
melts

12 mini pretzel twists

Green sprinkles

EQUIPMENT

Microwave-safe bowl

Microwave

Oven mitts

Wax paper

SHAMROCK PRETZELS

You don't have to find a patch of four-leaf clovers to get the luck of the Irish. Instead, make your own luck with this fun project. It's perfect for St. Patrick's Day or any time you feel the need for a green treat.

In a microwave-safe bowl, prepare the candy melts according to the package directions until they are smooth and runny. Remove from the microwave with oven mitts—the bowl will be hot!

Coat 3 mini pretzel twists in the candy and place on the wax paper in a triangle pattern to look like a shamrock. Break a curved piece off another pretzel twist for the stem. Coat in white candy and add it to the bottom of your shamrock. Repeat with the remaining pretzels.

Pour green sprinkles onto the shamrocks. Turn upside down to remove excess sprinkles and allow to harden.

DID YOU KNOW?

The first leaf of a shamrock represents hope, the second is for faith and the third is for love. And if there is a fourth, it represents luck, which is why four-leaf clovers are considered lucky.

It's Your Fantasy

There may be nothing that invokes your imagination more than mythical monsters and fantastical creatures found in fairy tales. From the time we are young, we grow up knowing the stories of brave knights who fought dragons and saved princesses.

In this chapter, you'll discover dragon eggs, crystal formations and royalty. You'll make your own wizard wand and dine like a fairy. Do you dare continue? (I think you do!)

MODERATE

UNICORN DESSERT CUPS

Enter the magical land of unicorns with a delicious treat, inspired by these magnificent creatures. This creamy dessert features a homemade unicorn horn that you can enjoy with your treat.

Unwrap the candies, place in a microwave-safe bowl and microwave on high for 5 to 10 seconds to soften them. Roll each color on the wax paper to create a rope. Twist the colors together and shape into a unicorn horn.

Layer the vanilla pudding and whipped cream in a cup and add the unicorn horn. Top with sprinkles.

DID YOU KNOW?
When Marco Polo first saw a rhinoceros, he thought it was a unicorn.

INGREDIENTS

4 colorful chewy candies, such as Starburst

½ cup (120 g) vanilla pudding

¼ cup (10 g) whipped cream

4 tbsp (60 g) sprinkles

EQUIPMENT

Microwave-safe bowl

Microwave

Oven mitts

Wax paper

Plastic cup

DRAGON EGGS

Enter the dragon's lair to uncover these colorful dragon eggs. Or just head to the kitchen and make your own!

Let's crack and color hard-boiled eggs to create a fun effect that resembles reptilian eggs. Just be sure not to go after their treasure.

NO ADULT SUPERVISION
REQUIRED

MODERATELY EASY

INGREDIENTS

6 hard-boiled eggs

Water

6 tsp (30 ml) vinegar

Food coloring: red, green, blue, purple, orange and pink

EQUIPMENT

6 cups

Spoon

Crack the outer shell of the eggs. Fill each cup halfway with water and add 1 teaspoon of vinegar and 4 drops of one food coloring to each cup. Stir well and add an egg to each cup.

Refrigerate overnight.

Remove the eggs from the cups and peel. Check out the colorful crack lines around the outside of the boiled eggs! So cool!

DID YOU KNOW?
Komodo dragons are the world's largest lizards.

CHOCOLATE GEODE

You don't have to explore a deep, dark cave to find a crystal geode. These rocks are the perfect addition to any fantasy playdate. They take a few days to grow, though, so be patient and you will end up with a sparkling treasure.

MODERATELY HARD

INGREDIENTS

3 cups (600 g) sugar

1 cup (235 ml) water

Blue food coloring

4 cups (500 g) all-purpose flour

½ cup (40 g) white candy melts

½ cup (40 g) light cocoa candy melts

EQUIPMENT

Saucepan

Stove

Large bowl

Small bowl

Aluminum foil

2 microwave-safe bowls

Microwave

Oven mitts

Cup

With a grown-up, stir together the sugar and water in a saucepan over medium heat until the sugar is fully dissolved. Remove from the heat and add 6 drops of the food coloring.

Place the flour in the large bowl and press the smaller bowl inside. Remove the small bowl and cover the flour in foil. This is the mold for the crystals of your geode. Pour the sugar solution into the mold. The flour will shift and allow the sugar solution to settle unevenly, which more closely mimics how crystals are formed naturally. Allow to harden for 48 hours.

After 48 hours, crystals will have formed as the sugar solution evaporates. There will still be liquid in the bowls, though. This can be discarded. Remove the foil backing from the candy geode. Turn your candy geode upside down and allow to dry for at least 12 hours.

In microwave-safe bowls, prepare each of the candy melts according to the package directions until they are smooth and runny. Remove from the microwave with oven mitts—the bowls will be hot! Place the dried-out candy geode over an upside-down cup and coat the back in white chocolate. Once the white candy has hardened, pour a layer of melted light cocoa on top.

DID YOU KNOW?

Table salt, snowflakes and pencil lead are all made up of crystals.

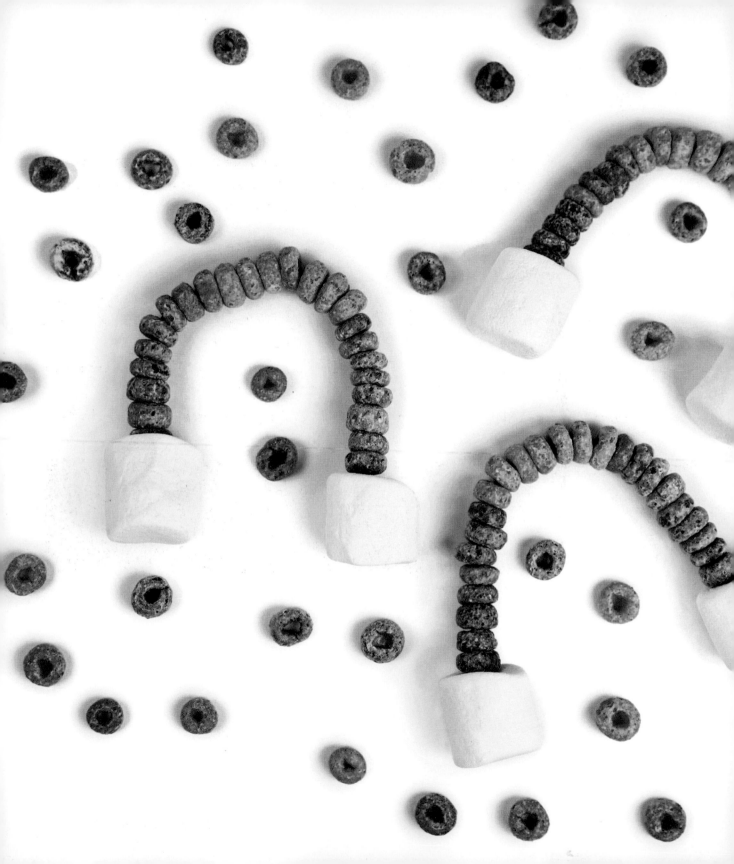

RAINBOW CEREAL CRAFT

Let's go somewhere over the rainbow with a fun treat everyone can enjoy. This project features a simple way to make a rainbow using cereal and candy. Talk about tasting the rainbow!

INGREDIENTS

1 cup (30 g) colorful ring cereal, such as Froot Loops

1 licorice string, such as Twizzlers PULL 'n' PEEL

2 jumbo marshmallows

EQUIPMENT

Wooden skewer

Sort your cereal into piles by color. It's okay to munch on a few as you sort!

Pull apart your string candy and thread it through your cereal. You can go in order of the colors of the rainbow (remember, ROY G. BIV—red, orange, yellow, green, blue, indigo, violet) or make your own rainbow by going in any order you like.

With a skewer, poke a hole in the top of a marshmallow and press the end of your rainbow into it to create a cloud. Now do it again on the other end.

See how long you can make your rainbow. Can you connect two strings together? Can you make it stand up?

DID YOU KNOW?

A rainbow isn't actually an object—it's an optical illusion! That means that no two people ever see the same rainbow! It appears differently for every person who sees it.

ADULT SUPERVISION
REQUIRED

MODERATE

WIZARD TOWER

Even the most powerful wizards need a place to call home. Build a fancy wizard tower from ice cream cones to begin your magical journey. Who knows—you might just slay a dragon along the way.

In a microwave-safe bowl, prepare the candy melts according to the package directions until they are smooth and runny. Remove from the microwave with oven mitts—the bowl will be hot!

Place in the zip-top bag and cut one of the corners to make a piping bag.

Use the melted candy to glue the bottoms of the sugar cones together. Line the opening of the waffle cone with melted candy and place on top of one of the sugar cones.

Let the tower set, then spray with silver color spray. Use the melted black candy to draw windows and doors onto the tower.

INGREDIENTS

½ cup (40 g) black candy melts

2 ice cream sugar cones

1 ice cream waffle cone

Edible silver color spray

EQUIPMENT

Microwave-safe bowl

Microwave

Oven mitts

Plastic zip-top bag

Scissors

DID YOU KNOW?
Castles were built to keep intruders out.

MODERATELY EASY

MUMMY PIZZA

Don't get wrapped up making plain old boring pizza. Mummy pizza is so much better! It's got all the ingredients of your favorite pizza with a spooktacular ingredient to bring out its mummy side. You can make these smaller versions for yourself or make a large one to share.

Preheat the oven to 400°F (200°C). Line a baking sheet with parchment paper.

Roll out the dough on a lightly floured surface. Cut out 8 mini pizzas with the cookie cutter. Spread 2 tablespoons (30 g) of the pizza sauce over each dough circle. Ask a grown-up to cut the string cheeses in half. You'll use one half for each pizza. Separate each string cheese into ribbons and lay across the pizza sauce. Place 2 sliced olives on each pizza for eyes.

Ask a grown-up to transfer the baking sheet to the oven and bake for 5 to 10 minutes, until the crust is golden brown.

INGREDIENTS

1 (1-lb [454-g]) package refrigerated pizza dough

Flour, for sprinkling

1 cup (240 g) pizza sauce

4 string cheese tubes

16 sliced olives

EQUIPMENT

Oven

Baking sheet

Parchment paper

Rolling pin

4" (10-cm) circle cookie cutter

Knife

DID YOU KNOW?
According to Egyptian mythology, the god Osiris was the very first mummy.

ADULT SUPERVISION REQUIRED

● ● ○ ○ ○

MODERATELY EASY

GHOST SANDWICHES

Boo! Make a batch of spooky ghost sandwiches, then gather a group of friends and share your favorite ghost stories. Grab a flashlight and make scary faces for even more fun.

With a butter knife, spread 2 tablespoons (30 g) of peanut butter on 6 slices of bread. Top with the remaining 6 slices of bread. With kitchen scissors, cut the sandwich into the shape of a ghost. Add 2 chocolate chips (with the smooth side out) for eyes and one for the mouth.

INGREDIENTS

¾ cup (180 g) peanut butter

12 pieces white sandwich bread

18 chocolate chips

EQUIPMENT

Butter knife

Kitchen scissors

DID YOU KNOW?

Prime Minister Winston Churchill claimed to have seen the ghost of Abraham Lincoln while staying in the White House.

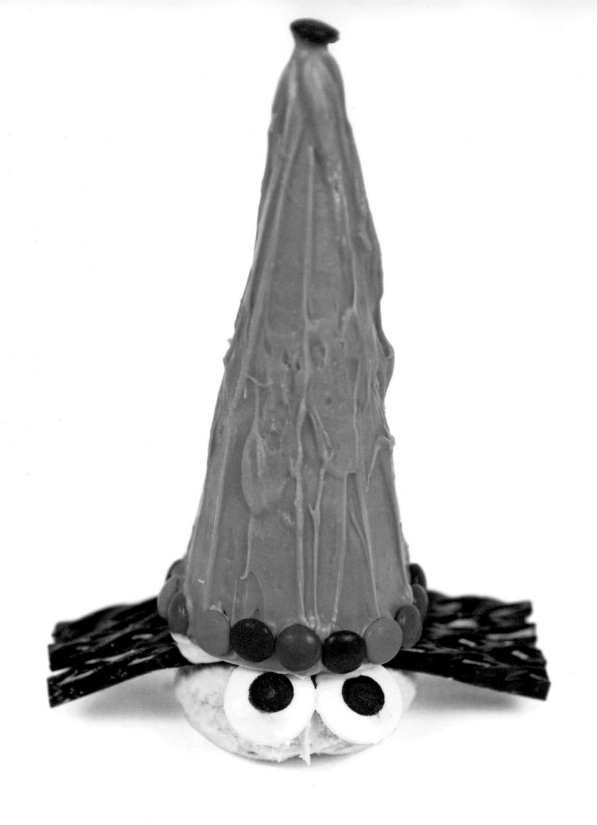

PRINCESS DESSERTS

You don't need a fairy godmother to whip up these princess desserts. Use your creativity to build a princess of your own. Then go enjoy the royal ball. Just don't get caught at midnight!

ADULT SUPERVISION REQUIRED

MODERATE

INGREDIENTS

¼ cup (20 g) pink candy melts

Ice cream cone

¼ cup (50 g) candy-coated chocolate drops, such as M&M's

3 black licorice laces

1 powdered doughnut

2 candy eyes

EQUIPMENT

Microwave-safe bowl

Microwave

Oven mitts

Paintbrush

Wax paper

Scissors

In a microwave-safe bowl, prepare the candy melts according to the package directions until they are smooth and runny. Remove from the microwave with oven mitts—the bowl will be hot!

Using a food-safe paintbrush, coat the outside of the ice cream cone with the melted candy. Line the opening of the ice cream cone with the chocolate-covered candies. Add another candy to the tip. Place on wax paper to harden.

Cut the licorice laces into small pieces. Use melted candy to attach the laces to the top of the powdered doughnut, like hair. Attach the candy eyes and place the waffle cone hat on top of the candy hair.

DID YOU KNOW?

Pocahontas is the only Disney princess based on a real person.

WIZARD WANDS

You don't have to wait for the wand to choose the wizard; make your own instead. These chocolate-covered wizard wands are the perfect magical treat. Use the caramel to create your own patterns and build a one-of-a-kind wand that would make any wizard jealous.

ADULT SUPERVISION REQUIRED

MODERATE

INGREDIENTS

3 caramel candies

3 pretzel rods

1 cup (80 g) dark cocoa candy melts

Edible gold dust

EQUIPMENT

2 microwave-safe bowls

Microwave

Oven mitts

Butter knife

Wax paper

Unwrap the caramel candies, put them in a microwave-safe bowl and place in the microwave on high for 10 to 15 seconds to soften. Remove from the microwave with oven mitts—the bowl will be hot!

Let the caramel cool a little, and then roll the caramel between your hands to create a long tube of candy. Wrap the caramel around the pretzel rods to make a spiral about three-fourths of the way down. You can also press it into the top of a pretzel rod to create the look of wood. You may not need all of the caramel.

In a microwave-safe bowl, prepare the candy melts according to the package directions until they are smooth and runny. Remove from the microwave with oven mitts—the bowl will be hot!

Dip the pretzel wands into the melted candy. Coat them completely and use a butter knife to smooth the bottom one-fourth to make it look like a handle.

Set on wax paper and sprinkle with gold dust. Once the wands have set, they're ready to use!

DID YOU KNOW?

Daniel Radcliffe wore out 60 to 70 wands during the making of the *Harry Potter* films.

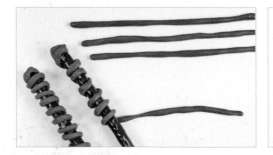

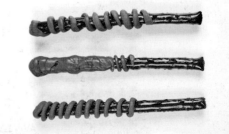

ADULT SUPERVISION
REQUIRED

MODERATE

FAIRY SANDWICH

This fairy sandwich is something that I imagine fairies would enjoy. It's whimsical and fun, with an extra special surprise. Try cutting out different shapes or using different sprinkles to make your own fairy snack.

Use the cookie cutter to cut a shape from the corner of a piece of bread. Spread the peanut butter onto another slice of bread and press them together.

Add the sprinkles to the cutout piece and lightly press to secure them in place. Turn upside down to remove excess sprinkles.

INGREDIENTS

2 slices white sandwich bread

2 tbsp (30 g) peanut butter

1 tsp rainbow sprinkles

EQUIPMENT

Star- or heart-shaped cookie cutter

Butter knife

DID YOU KNOW?

Fairy gardens are cute little gardens with miniature accessories made to attract fairies.

In the Garden

Nature is one of the greatest works of art. Just look out your window and you can see the beauty of the world around you—in the trees lining the sidewalk, in the garden you pass by on the way to school.

This chapter features projects with a garden theme. We'll make butterflies, caterpillars and sunflowers. We'll build a terrace lined with roses. And we'll make lollipops filled with real flowers that you can actually eat.

Don't just stop to smell the roses—make some!

BUTTERFLY PRETZELS

ADULT SUPERVISION
REQUIRED

● ● ● ○ ○

MODERATE

My son once told me that there are two kinds of bugs—good bugs and bad bugs. I think butterflies definitely fall into the good bug category. They are pretty, not scary. They help plants grow. And now, you can enjoy this "good bug" with a twist all your own. Use yummy chocolate candies to create different patterns on your butterflies. Can you recreate any that you've seen in the real world?

INGREDIENTS

1 cup (80 g) candy melts in your favorite color

6 pretzel sticks

12 pretzel twists

36 candy-coated chocolate drops, such as M&M's

EQUIPMENT

Microwave-safe bowl

Microwave

Oven mitts

Wax paper

Spoon

In a microwave-safe bowl, prepare the candy melts according to the package directions until they are smooth and runny. Remove from the microwave with oven mitts—the bowl will be hot!

Coat a pretzel stick in the melted candy. Place on wax paper and attach 2 pretzel twists to the side to create a butterfly body and wings. Spoon melted candy onto the top of the prezel twist wings.

Add chocolate candies to your butterfly to create patterns. Draw antennae with the melted candy. Repeat with the remaining ingredients to make 5 more butterflies.

DID YOU KNOW?
Butterflies taste things with their feet.

NO ADULT SUPERVISION
REQUIRED

MODERATELY EASY

CHOCOLATE SUNFLOWERS

Don't sunflowers just make you happy? These big, bright flowers are as fun to make as they are to find. And this edible version is the best kind because you can enjoy them with all your senses—not just your eyes.

INGREDIENTS

¼ cup (60 g) yellow frosting

6 cylindrical chocolate-covered caramel candies, such as Rolo

1 (7.5-oz [212-g]) package candy-coated sunflower seeds

EQUIPMENT

Butter knife

With a butter knife, spread frosting on the outside of the caramel candies. Press the sunflower seeds onto the icing to form petals for the sunflowers.

DID YOU KNOW?
The world's tallest sunflower was grown in Germany and was 27 feet (8.2 m) tall.

NO ADULT SUPERVISION
REQUIRED

EASY

CATERPILLAR GRAPE SKEWERS

This hungry, hungry caterpillar is the perfect snack for a busy day. It's super easy to make, too.

Try freezing the finished skewers for a yummy, cold treat on hot summer days.

INGREDIENTS

6 green grapes

6 purple grapes

1 tsp melted white chocolate

2 mini chocolate chips

1 mini pretzel stick

EQUIPMENT

Bamboo skewer

Thread the green and purple grapes in alternating colors onto the bamboo skewer until the skewer is filled. Use the melted white chocolate to attach chocolate chips to the top grape for eyes.

Break the pretzel stick into small pieces and attach to the top grape to create antennae.

DID YOU KNOW?
A caterpillar's first meal is usually its eggshell.

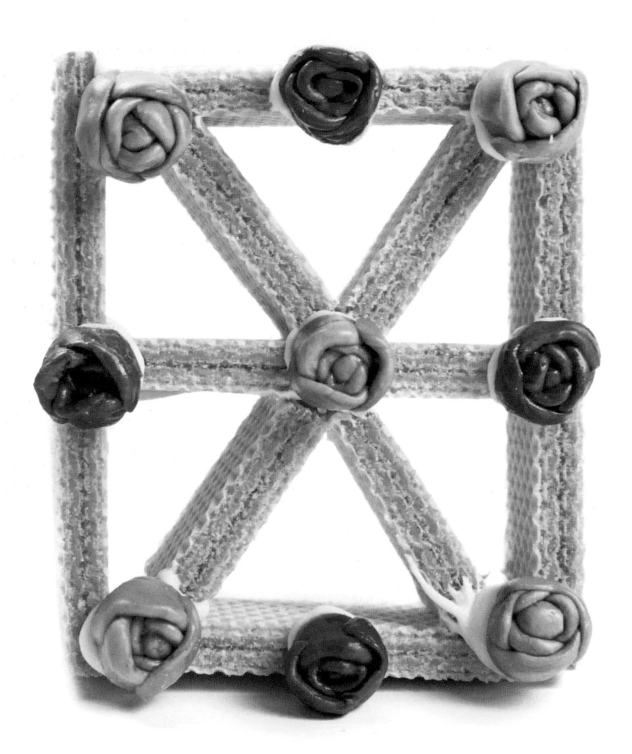

FLOWER TERRACE

Here's a garden that doesn't need sunshine or water to grow. Instead, you just need some imagination and creativity! What color will you make your flowers? See how high you can build your terrace. What shapes work better for the inside structure of the terrace?

And when you're done building, don't forget to enjoy this delicious treat.

ADULT SUPERVISION
REQUIRED

MODERATELY HARD

INGREDIENTS

10 colorful chewy candies, such as Starburst

½ cup (40 g) white candy melts

6 vanilla wafer cookies

EQUIPMENT

Microwave-safe bowl

Microwave

Oven mitts

Wax paper

Place the wrapped candies in a microwave-safe bowl. Microwave on high for 5 to 10 seconds to soften them. Remove from the microwave with oven mitts—the bowl will be hot! Unwrap the candies and press them flat with the palm of your hand.

Tear a small piece of candy and roll into a ball to make the center of your rose. Tear off more pieces of candy and shape into petals. Press them into the outside of the rose, moving around the flower as you go.

Repeat with other colors to make several roses.

In a microwave-safe bowl, prepare the candy melts according to the package directions until they are smooth and runny. Remove from the microwave with oven mitts—the bowl will be hot!

Build a terrace using the vanilla wafer cookies. Lay 2 side by side vertically on the wax paper. Cut another wafer cookie into smaller pieces and attach them diagonally using the melted candy.

Attach the roses using the melted candy.

> ### DID YOU KNOW?
> Broccoli is actually a flower!

BIRD'S NESTS

I adore the sound of birds chirping. It means there's life outside. It means the world is moving on. It means adventure awaits.

There may not be any chirping birds in these marshmallow bird's nests, but I think I can let that slide. How about you?

ADULT SUPERVISION REQUIRED

MODERATELY EASY

INGREDIENTS

¼ cup (56 g) unsalted butter

2 cups (90 g) mini marshmallows

4 cups (180 g) chow mein noodles

36 candy eggs

EQUIPMENT

Saucepan

Stove

Large mixing bowl

Spoon

Muffin pan

Nonstick cooking spray

In a small saucepan, melt the butter and marshmallows over medium-high heat. Add the chow mein noodles to a large mixing bowl. Pour the butter and marshmallow mixture over the noodles and stir to coat.

Spray the muffin pan with nonstick cooking spray and press the noodle mixture into the muffin molds. Create an indention in the middle of each muffin cavity to create a nest shape.

Allow to cool, then place 3 candy eggs inside each nest.

DID YOU KNOW?
Many birds glue their nests together with spiderwebs, saliva and mud.

ADULT SUPERVISION
REQUIRED

EASY

EDIBLE FLOWER LOLLIPOPS

Did you know that you could eat some flowers? Well, now you do. So if you're ever lost in the wilderness, a flower might save your life.

Or you could just make these gorgeous edible flower lollipops. It's probably safer.

INGREDIENTS

24 clear peppermint candies

Pressed edible flowers

EQUIPMENT

Oven

Plastic zip-top bag

Mallet

Lollipop mold

Baking sheet

Oven mitts

6 lollipop sticks

Airtight storage container

Preheat the oven to 250°F (120°C).

Unwrap the peppermint candies, place in a plastic bag and smash with the mallet.

Add a flower or petals to each cavity of the lollipop mold. Pour the smashed candy on top of the flowers. Place the lollipop mold on a baking sheet and ask a grown-up to transfer it to the oven. Bake for 15 to 30 minutes, until the candy has completely melted.

Have a grown-up remove the baking sheet from the oven with oven mitts and press a lollipop stick into the back of each lollipop, twisting it once to coat it in the candy.

Allow the lollipops to harden before removing them from the mold.

Store in an airtight container.

DID YOU KNOW?
In the 1600s, tulip flowers were worth more than gold!

Acknowledgments

First, a huge thank-you to my husband, James, for encouraging me to chase my crazy dreams. I could not have asked for a better partner in this journey.

To Andrew, my inspiration in life: Thank you for filling my days with light and teaching me what it means to be a mom.

To my parents, Danny and Nancy: You taught me that I could do anything I set my mind to and never let me settle for "good enough." I am so lucky to be your daughter.

To Lonnie, Leslie and Kate: Thanks for the love and support you've shown me as you welcomed me into your family. And for loving my baby boy as much as you do.

To Holly, an amazing mentor and friend: I'm so glad you did not bat an eye when I confided that I wanted to write a book, but instead said, "Let's make it happen."

I am forever grateful to Jet, Brad, Jamie and Spencer who let me "borrow" their children to fill the pages of this project. Thanks to Mrs. Sauce's kindergarten class for stretching their imaginations and creating the most beautiful coloring book cookies I could have hoped for.

And thanks to Will, Marissa and the entire team at Page Street for the chance to fulfill my lifelong dream of becoming a published author.

About the Author

Arena Blake used to spend her days in the White House writing about the president. Now she spends her days at the kitchen table writing about kids crafts and activities. She shares creative projects, recipes and the exploits of her nerdy family at TheNerdsWife.com.

Arena lives in Fort Worth, Texas, with her husband and son.

Index